# Out of the Attic

A MEMOIR

PAMELA SPOCK

The content of this book reflects the author's recollections and otherwise interpretations of events. While every effort has been made to ensure accuracy, some names and details have been changed or omitted to protect privacy. For questions, contact: pamspock@gmail.com

**With deep gratitude to my editor friends: Sylvia Moore, Lynette Woods, and Jack and Karen Helser for their insightful edits and steady encouragement.**

Cover photo by Olga Andriyash, used with permission.

ISBN: 979-8-9989724-1-6 (Paperback)
ISBN: 979-8-9989724-2-3 (eBook)

Library of Congress Control Number: 2025910402

Out of the Attic: a memoir
Published by Pamela Spock, Canandaigua, N.Y.
Printed in the United States of America

First edition 2025

# Contents

*Dedications* — v

*Introduction* — vii

1. Window to the World — 1
2. The Easter Parade — 7
3. A Top-Secret Mission — 15
4. The Old Rugged Cross — 29
5. Opening a Pandora's Box — 39
6. The Search for a Sign — 45
7. Aunt Ethel — 51
8. Solomon and the Half-Baby — 59
9. Last Words — 65
10. A City in Turmoil — 71
11. Freddy Flad — 79
12. Fanny Farmer — 87
13. Double-Take — 93
14. Back From the Dead — 97
15. A Polish Boy — 101
16. Getting the Blessing — 109
17. Goodbye Dolly — 117
18. The Last Straw — 123
19. Love Notes — 133
20. The Heat Is On — 141
21. Seed on Good Soil — 145
22. A Divine Touch — 151
23. Migrant Work — 155
24. Excommunication — 161
25. Ride in a Police Car — 165
26. Mildred Sr — 173

27. Rocky, Rocky Mountains                    179
28. Growing Pains                             189
29. Amazing Grace                             193
30. End of the World                          199
31. The Hunt Resumes                          207
32. Surprised by God                          213
33. A Horde of Hugs                           217
34. Golden Years                              223
    Epilogue                                  229

    *You Can Know*                            234
    *More Information*                        235

*Dedications...*

Dedicated to my two half-siblings,
who went home early.
I look forward to meeting you
for the first time someday.

And to Anne VanPatten,
for her "lost and found" gift.
Anne—your role in my mother's story
was nothing short of miraculous.

*Introduction*

"*The fact that our heart yearns for something earth can't supply, is proof that heaven must be our home.*"

— C.S. LEWIS

How do we understand the value of a person's life? Is it like a beautiful flower on a mountaintop that is unseen and gone too soon? Or is it like a bestselling novel that is celebrated for a season, then left to gather dust on a thrift-store shelf? Or is every life—no matter how brief—an essential thread in a divinely woven tapestry, with its stories destined to be told and retold around eternity's campfires?

I didn't fully appreciate the woman whose story you're about to read, at least not at first. It took some years for her to become my dearest friend, as well as my mother. Sometimes she would share stories from her childhood that left me amused, heartbroken, or in awe—but I didn't know how they all fit together. Like me, her life was still unfolding.

When my mother was older, however, a surprising "plot twist" occurred. That's when friends and family suggested her story should be written down... or at least submitted to Oprah's talk show!

Now, eight years after her death, Millie's story is being told. Naturally, I wish I'd done it while she was still alive. I could have confirmed every detail, explored every emotion, and ensured her experiences were accurately portrayed. Instead, I had to rely on my memory of conversations and events, along with months of research, interviews, and poring over old photographs, notes, and letters.

For what I don't remember—or know for certain—I've taken creative liberties. This includes rearranging or combining some events and, like a puzzle with a few missing pieces, coloring in the gaps as best I could.

I'm sure this book would've been different had my mom written it. However, as her daughter, (and someone who shared a special bond with her) I feel hopeful I've captured the spirit of Millie's life, along with its most significant details.

I also wrote it from the standpoint that Millie's story is, at its core, everyone's story. From the moment we're born, we begin a journey "home." Along the way we experience joys, sorrows, adventures, and costly lessons. We're *all* challenged to break free from the lies that imprison us and to discover the true meaning of family, belonging, and, most importantly... *Love.*

This journey to freedom and discovery is what Millie's life was all about. And now, I invite you to turn the page and discover your own story in hers...

— Pamela Spock

# CHAPTER 1

# Window to the World

On a bleak afternoon, a seven-year-old girl leaned on a window ledge in an equally bleak attic. Chin in on hand and a piece of chalk in the other, she pressed her chubby cheek against the rain-spotted glass.

*I don't hate Leo,* she thought, straining to see a sliver of blue above the dark city landscape. *Why do I have to hate Leo?*

Not everything was dismal for Millie Saxe, though. At least there was a window in her attic bedroom, a place to watch the world go by and "dream away the dreary day," as her mother often sang on Saint Patrick's Day:

*I rose up in the morning and I felt a dire need*
*To dream away the dreary day and down a cup of mead.*
*I felt the sting of honeybees, from last night's revelry*
*I'm looking for the honey that'll cure my soul's disease.*

Recalling this song, Millie clutched the chalk even tighter. Like any child, she longed for the sweetness of a carefree life—one that preserved her innocence and filled her days with laughter and smiles.

But this wasn't the world she was born into. All around her, even within her body, bees buzzed; stinging bees that seemed intent on keeping this kind of life just out of reach.

Still, for a little while, she tried wishing for a better life on a small patch of green—like a child wishing on a star—that she saw from her window. In the center of a pine grove stood a tall, solitary tree that was dead and spindly. A large bird often perched on one of its branches, and sometimes, when the late-morning sun warmed the air, it would spread its wings and freeze like a Halloween decoration. Her mother said the bird was an osprey; Millie argued it was an eagle. Whatever it was, she was certain that if she concentrated hard enough, it would leap from the branch and soar!

Like many post-war cities, Rochester—New York's "Flower City"—was booming in 1947, the year Millie was born, and its concrete jungle kept growing. Major companies such as Eastman Kodak, Xerox, and Bausch & Lomb were rooted there, along with countless smaller businesses, all needing workers, and workers needing housing. One such solution appeared in the form of a high-rise apartment building that sprang up suddenly, blocking Millie's view of the skyline.

Overnight, her green grove of dreams disappeared.

Millie stepped back from the window and opened her fist, letting the chalk fall to the wooden floor. For a moment, she noticed little half-moon fingernail indents in her palm. Before they disappeared, she counted them. *Four.*

That reminded her of something. She hadn't counted the sentences yet. Walking over to the blackboard fixed to the wall, she slowly counted each one.

*I hate Leo. One. I hate Leo. Two. I hate Leo. Three....*

Repeatedly, the same sentence was counted until she reached the end. *Fifty-three.* Her mother had told her to write it fifty times, so Millie opened a drawer in her dresser and pulled out a sock. Then she spat on it and used it to erase the last three sentences.

Leo was Millie's father—or so she thought. Once, when she was five, she called him "dad" and got whopped under the chin by her mother. When "dad" slipped out again this time, however, all hell broke loose. Her mother, whose large frame rarely made it up the stairs, chased a fleeing Millie up every step, screaming, "Dad? Don't you call him Dad! He's not worthy of being a father!" That's when she gave Millie the blackboard assignment, before returning downstairs to scream and bawl for the rest of the afternoon.

Millie looked up at the completed, shameful board. *Hate. Hate.* What sharp, distasteful words! They filled her eyes, and then her mouth, like glass shards. She felt her tongue swell. She put it between her teeth and squeezed down hard, feeling the discomfort of the pressure on its flesh.

*I wish I couldn't speak,* she thought, wincing. Sometimes she was a good girl for saying something bad, and other times a bad girl for saying something good. Maybe if she bit off her tongue, that would fix everything?

Fortunately, a runny nose distracted her from trying. She wiped it on her sleeve and wandered over to a bookcase. Its shelves were decorated with horses and white picket fences and taped behind them were torn-out magazine pages of farms and nature scenes.

"There, there," Millie sniffled, stroking the mane of a Breyer mare, "everything's gonna be okay."

She then picked up other horses from the shelf: tiny ones, furry ones, broken ones, even unicorns (as they mostly looked like horses).

"And for you too, and for you..." she repeated, acknowledging and comforting each one before placing them back.

Millie loved animals, but horses had her heart. Maybe it started when she saw Sally Starr on television, galloping across the field on

Pal, her palomino horse. A large, beautiful beast that could take a little girl anywhere? It stirred a deep sense of freedom and power in Millie. Every time Sally ended her show with, *"May the Good Lord be blessing you and your family,"* Millie mouthed an *"amen."*

Walking to the corner, Millie picked up Dolly, her stick horse, and trotted around the room. Ever since her third-grade teacher mentioned the idea, she had pined for riding lessons.

"You don't have to get me any other Christmas presents!" she had pleaded with her mother one day, not at all worried if the bargaining worked. She never got what she wanted anyway—except for Ladybug, a Jack Russell Terrier puppy she received on her sixth birthday (but who wasn't allowed up in the attic). Usually, her mother just bought dolls, stuffed animals, or games that required someone else to play with.

*Seven is old enough for a grown-up gift,* Millie reasoned. If she had a real horse, she could be like Sally Starr. She could be strong, independent, and free!

Noticing it had grown dark outside, Millie put her toys away and sat on the bed. Her tummy was grumbling, and the house was quiet. Should she go downstairs? Figuring out her mother's moods was never easy.

She let out a deep sigh. Right then, more than anything—*even more than riding a real horse*—Millie wished she had a brother or sister.

*How fun it would be,* she thought, *to hang out together in the attic, play games, and "dream away the dreary days" together!*

But that wish was fading. Not even the Sibley's Santa whose lap she sat on every year could make *that* wish come true.

Suddenly, a creak of an opening door interrupted the attic's silence. The smell of spaghetti sauce on the stove and Wonder Bread in the toaster wafted up the stairwell.

"Millie? Come down now," her mother called up, a slight tremble in her voice. "I've made supper. Come eat."

Millie jumped up and exhaled. The storm was over. She smoothed her checkered wool skirt and yanked up her slipping leotards.

"Coming!" she called. Then she hesitated in front of the blackboard. She suddenly felt a strong urge to erase the words—and the memory—of her confusing day.

She picked up the sock from the ledge and held it for a moment. Then she set it back down.

*I'll erase it later,* she decided, heading for the stairs. If she didn't hurry, her mother's mood might change again.

# CHAPTER 2

# The Easter Parade

The following year, after Millie turned eight, Easter burst forth like a racehorse out of a gate. Frost melted. Robins sang. Crocuses and daffodils threw off their soil-covered blankets. The whole world seemed eager to leave winter behind.

Millie started the morning by using the downstairs bathroom. Outside the door, her mother was serenading her:

"Here comes Peter Cottontail, hopping down the bunny trail. Hippity-hoppity, Easter's now today!"

When Millie came out, her mother caught her by the shoulder.

"Hop to it, missy. Breakfast first. Then you've got *three* baskets to find!"

Millie skipped to the kitchen, already knowing the plan. Holidays in her home were like penny balloons: cheap but inflated. And her mother, more stable around the holidays, had a way of pumping out the magic. Decorations, special foods, goofy songs... by the time the day arrived, you felt *sure* to explode!

"Then we have to put on your dress for church," her mother continued, her arm held high, pouring a stream of syrup onto a mountain of pancakes.

*Whoosh!* The excitement instantly drained out of Millie. Her shoulders slumped. Why did she always have to wear those home-made dresses? They were scratchy, girly, and kids didn't need another reason to laugh at her.

Millie swallowed her complaint (along with her pancakes) to focus on her baskets. When she found them, she dumped them out, sifting through the plastic grass to make sure every chocolate egg and jellybean was accounted for.

There were toys among the loot as well—the largest one being a felted tin rabbit that played a drum. Before she could wind it up, her mother pulled her aside. There was no escape... the dress was coming down over her head.

"Stop it!" her mother barked, yanking at the collar from behind. "You're wiggling like a cat on hot bricks!"

Millie winced as her mother's iron grip pinched the back of her neck. Then she pushed out her stomach, hoping the dress would split.

"What the—" her mother sputtered. "That's odd. It fit last week. Must be the humidity."

As she reached for her dress shears, she knocked over a small end table and spilled out an expletive. "Leo, pick that up for me. Hurry up!"

Leo, who had been cleaning all morning, set down his feather duster.

"Yes, Toots," he answered, dropping to his hands and feet.

He then crawled around gathering pins and sewing notions from the carpet. Seeing the old shirt and dungarees he was wearing, Millie knew he was staying home. She sighed. They only went to church on holidays, but for some reason Leo *never* had to go!

"Mother, can we take your car to church today? *Pleeaaase?*" Millie looked sideways for a reaction. Another hard yank on the dress.

"Don't be stupid. You know it's only two blocks away."

She should've known it was knew it was useless to ask.

Her mother's tradition of walking to church wasn't about practicality. It was a chance to be in a *parade*. A parade that started at their front door, headed east on Webster Avenue, turned a corner at the Italian meat market, and after a short meander through a WWII memorial garden, concluded by marching down the aisle of the Methodist Church.

*It's a good thing I don't have wheels,* Millie thought, nearly giggling at the image in her mind. *Mother would turn me into a float!*

"There," Toots said, turning Millie around. She was clearly pleased with herself for using a bread wire to fasten the button to the buttonhole. "That'll have to do. Look at her, Leo. Isn't my little girl the spitting image of Shirley Temple?"

Leo didn't answer. He barely looked up. Toots walked over to her handbag and snatched a slip of paper from its pocket.

"Oh, sugar, I forgot this."

She stuffed the paper into a plastic egg on the table and tossed it to Millie across the room.

Millie wasn't quick enough. The egg bounced off her fingertip and rolled under the television console.

"Quick. Get it. I don't have all day."

Millie rushed for the egg, retrieved the paper, and read it aloud:

*This certificate entitles the bearer, <u>Mildred A. Saxe</u> to receive <u>Six Beginner Riding Lessons</u>, at <u>Heberle's Young Rider Stables</u>, <u>Rochester, N.Y.</u>*

Millie shrieked and ran to hug her mother.

"Oh, thank you, thank you!" she gushed, the ruffles on her dress flouncing with every bounce.

Toots patted Millie on the head and pushed her away at the same time.

*Is she annoyed by my excitement? Or because the dress is too small?* Millie didn't care. *Hyah! Sally Starr, here I come!*

Toots pulled two raincoats from the closet, holding the smaller one out to Millie.

"You can also thank my sister," she said curtly. "She paid half."

During the walk, Millie bubbled over with questions. "When can I start? What kind of horse will I ride? Will I have a silver saddle?"

Toots tightened her grip on Millie's hand.

"Don't scuff your Mary Janes," she replied.

They passed the home of Barbara Slater, the president of the P.T.A. She was out sweeping her porch.

"Happy Easter, Toots! Thanks again for the cupcakes last week. We hope to see you at the next committee meeting!"

Toots waved back and beamed, then resumed the click-clack march of her wedge heels pounding the sidewalk. A woman of stature to begin with, a good compliment always seemed to grow her another inch.

Millie glanced up at her. Her mother filled out a polka-dotted dress with silver buttons; her short, curled hair wrapped tightly in a scarf. Even in profile, her plain features were cagey and intense. Her steel-gray eyes, with unusually small pupils, had a way of unsettling you if you stared too long into them—although you couldn't say exactly why.

Millie suddenly wondered something.

"Did you used to play the trumpet?" she asked. "Is that why your name is Toots?"

Her mother shot a quick, perturbed glance.

"No," she answered. "It's a nickname I got as a teenager when... oh, you never mind. You know my real name is Mildred. We both got our names from my mother. You also get your middle name from her."

"I know, Anna Banana." Millie giggled. She wished Anna was her first name. She also wished her grandmother was alive and not just a woman in a photograph. Kids with grandparents were so lucky!

Toots looked down. "You're going to name your baby girl Mildred, too, aren't you?"

A lump formed in Millie's throat. The question touched a nerve, and not just because she hated the name Mildred.

"C-could I?" she stammered. "Have a baby?"

Sadly, her mother failed to notice Millie's face, and how it was darkened with a worry that a little girl her age should never have.

Toots lit up when they reached the church.

"Well, well!" she cackled at the line going in the door. "Look at everyone all gussied up in their pretty Easter clothes!"

She said it loud enough for people to turn and stare. Millie walked into church with her head lowered, only to become a spectacle once again to a row of beady-eyed, snickering siblings. Two of the girls she recognized from a neighbor-hood block party, where they had played hopscotch together. She had even foolishly thought of them as friends.

Millie slipped into the pew and slouched down. *What's wrong with me?* she wondered. *Why is everyone so mean to me?*

As the congregation sang hymns, a miserable tune played in Millie's head. She looked around the sanctuary. Tall stained-glass windows depicted fractured, confusing scenes from the Bible. In the pews, colorfully dressed women in Easter bonnets and men with suit coats and ties sat rigidly, like statues. By their sides sat more restless children—children lucky enough to have siblings to play with, banter with, and tease other children with.

Even the words from the pulpit, like "God's love" and "resurrection," were hard to grasp, floating in her mind like fragile, popping bubbles. Millie wasn't raised religious. On a good day her mother might read her a Bible story from a picture book. Or play hymns on the record player. Anyone who knew Toots well, though, knew how irreligious she could be. Catch her at a bad time, and her lack of piety could make an atheist blush!

Millie looked down at her puffy arms and legs wrapped in a concoction of lemon chiffon taffeta and white lace. Who was she, anyway? Her mother's daughter, of course. That much seemed clear —her mother never let her forget. Hanging prominently in the living room was Millie's framed birth certificate, plainly listing Mildred as her mother and Leo as her father.

Plus, countless times Millie had heard about the agonizing pain she'd caused her mother in childbirth. Toots would tell other women about it with such melodrama, that Millie didn't know if she should feel special or guilty.

*No wonder she had pain,* Millie thought, *if I was this fat when I came out!*

The service ended and people flooded into the center aisle to leave. Toots chatted with those around her, reveling in the compliments she received about Millie's dress.

A hapless man then made a passing remark about the Army and Senator McCarthy hearings. Without a second thought about whether it was appropriate for church, Toots released Millie's hand and launched into her opinion on communist sympathizers. She spoke with both hands, waving and clapping them together to drive her point home.

Millie took the chance to slip behind her. An elderly woman walked alongside, keeping pace.

"Hello, dear. Nice to see you this morning."

Millie smiled, amused by the woman's hat. A bouquet of fresh flowers was mounted on top, looking as though they were growing out of her head!

The woman extended her palm.

"Happy Easter!" she said, slipping something into Millie's hand. "Here's a little gift for you."

It was a small advertising button—the metal kind with a pin on the back. Flipping it over, Millie read: *"I'm OK, God Doesn't Make Junk."*

She looked up to mumble thanks, but the woman had disappeared. Only her hat could be seen—the bouquet, that is—drifting and bobbing along until it eventually became absorbed into the sea of hats and heads.

*A little corny,* Millie thought, as she slipped the button into her pocket. It wasn't as mighty as her lady sheriff pin, nor as bragworthy as her official Mouseketeer badge. But even so, there was something about the silly little button that comforted her. She found herself gripping it the entire walk home, and once in the attic, she placed it on the stand next to her bed where she could see it.

It carried a message she so desperately wanted to believe.

# CHAPTER 3

# A Top-Secret Mission

Millie groaned at the bright summer sun blazing through her window. It hovered just above the building where her grove of dreams used to be. She threw off her blanket, sending a circus of stuffed animals flying through the air.

"Oh no! I overslept!" she cried. Rushing to her dresser, she pulled a sheet off a birdcage. "Blinky, I'll feed you when I get back!"

The yellow parakeet inside didn't make a peep. Much like Leo, Blinky wasn't much of a talker.

Then Millie accidentally kicked something. It was her ladybug house. She carefully picked up the red box by its handle.

"Oops, sorry, ladies," she cooed into a little screened window.

The red dots inside were unnamed, but Millie had rescued each one from the threat of Toots's Kirby vacuum. The gentlest way— learned from lots of practice—was to pick them up using a moistened wad of tissue.

After placing the box in a sunbeam streaked across her bed, she walked over to a darkly stained dresser. Her mother had found it discarded alongside the street, insisting Leo and her uncle carry it upstairs. "It's an antique, made of walnut!" she said, likely expecting more appreciation.

But Millie didn't understand the value of old things. She was only nine. Nor did she care if it was made of nuts. She only knew that its ugly drawers—with handles shaped like gargoyles—looked better after she had plastered them with her entire collection of Looney Tunes stickers.

The dresser was also the place where she put her hermit crab tank. Their neighbor Trudy—who also had crabs—had given Millie the tank, along with four little crabs. Immediately, Millie put her interior decorating skills to work. By simply adding sand, seashells, silk flowers, and a Barbie doll sunbathing on a dishrag, she transformed a conventional tank into a cool and colorful Copacabana for her crustaceans.

As hurried as she was, she just *had* to peek inside.

"Still the same," she muttered. Crabs one through four still had their numbers written on their shells with a magic marker, while two unmarked shells remained empty.

She tapped on the glass. "Come on, crabbies, I know you can do it!"

To most people, hermit crabs were dull as dishwater. But Millie knew something special about them. Without warning, a crab could suddenly emerge from its shell and scurry into an empty, larger one. The first time Millie saw one of Trudy's crabs streak its ugly, naked body across the tank, she was horrified! Now she couldn't wait to see it happen again—with one of her own.

Millie pulled out some clothes from the top drawer. Then, as fast as Wonder Woman twirled into her super-hero outfit, she changed into hers: stretchy pedal pushers and an oversized T-shirt.

She caught a glimpse of herself in the mirror.

"Tomboy!" she heard. It was Jennifer Longberry's voice in her head. Jennifer was Millie's mortal enemy in grade school: a girl who could wear dresses *and* look pretty in them.

Millie ran her fingers through her long brown hair. She was a bit shorter than average, but not by much. Her smooth, white complexion showcased full lips and well-balanced features. When her hair used to be shorter and pin-curled by her mother, she *did* resemble Shirley Temple. Strangers would say it to her all the time.

One feature she did like about herself was her blue eyes—perfectly spaced and bright. She was, even to herself, "almost pretty," except for...

She turned to the side for a longer look in the mirror. *Except for these rolls!*

Tugging at her loose T-shirt, she wondered whether it hid or only highlighted what she hated most about herself. When and why she'd put on so much weight, she couldn't remember. Was it because of... *him?* The truth was, she was heavy before he made her do those things. She was even chubby in her baby pictures.

Millie stopped herself. No time for fighting the demons in her head. She snatched a yellow ribbon and tied her hair in a big bow. Yes, a little feminine, but she needed all the brownie points she could get with her mother.

She pinched her cheeks. "Okay, gang. I'm ready to get this show on the road!"

Silence. Blinky just blinked. The crabs kept sleeping. And the ladybugs, well, they didn't make a sound either.

She'd take care of her zoo later. For now, it was time for her secret mission. The plans were in place. The day had come. And any minute now Aunt Mabel would be dropping off her son, Patrick—who, it had already been decided, would make the *perfect* accomplice.

Millie bounced down the stairs into the living room.

"Good morning, Leo," she said cheerfully. "Where's Mother?"

Leo sat in his chair, brooding in a cloud of spiced cherry tobacco. A rattling fan nearby was struggling to blow the smoke out the window. He set his pipe down and pointed toward the kitchen.

Through the back screen door, Millie caught a glimpse of Toots tending her roses. She was nearly invisible, her mottled green dress and smock blending perfectly into a row of well-trimmed boxwoods.

"Moocho grasses," Millie said, practicing some Spanish she'd learned in school. She grabbed a canister of fish food and tucked it into the elastic waistband of her pants.

Despite the fact he rarely spoke to her, Millie liked Leo. Toots called him "Mouse," but Millie thought of him as a lion—at least when it came to work. He held down two jobs, plus an endless honey-do list at home. And even though she couldn't call him "Dad," he was kind to her, like a good dad should be.

It wasn't until Millie was older that she learned more about Leo. He'd been married once before, but his wife had died. Then, when he married Toots a year before Millie was born, it caught everyone by surprise. Leo was twenty-five years older than Toots, had been her uncle by marriage, and—according to rumor—he was Toots's third marriage.

Neither had children from their previous marriages.

Millie couldn't help but hover at Leo's side. It was rare to see the man resting. When you did, you almost didn't want to breathe. Usually, he'd be in his armchair, pipe in hand, trying to catch a bit of news on a small black-and-white television set on a table in front of him. He was especially obsessed with the space program and its plans for a moon landing. Whenever it was mentioned, he came alive; his old, tired face transformed into that of a little boy. It glowed so brightly, in fact, that watching him return to his normal self was unnerving... like watching the moon eclipse the sun.

Millie noticed the Band-Aid on his face.

"How's your cheek?" she asked hesitantly. She suddenly worried he might be angry with her for what had recently happened. At first, it had seemed like just another of Toots's outbursts, but when Millie arrived on the scene, she knew it was worse than usual. Leo had crawled under the settee, trying to shield himself from Toots's kicks. Then, when an upholstery staple sliced his cheek, Millie panicked and rushed to the neighbors for help—ultimately leading to the police being called.

Leo looked at Millie with his good eye. The other, damaged by cataract surgery, was crossed.

"Fine, fine. Now go see your mother."

As he spoke, he patted Millie's arm lightly with his calloused fingers. The small gesture made her feel better. She skipped off to the back door.

"Good morning," Millie blurted out, suddenly appearing behind her mother.

Toots bolted upright and dropped her pruning snips. "Dammit, Millie. Don't do that. What are you doing, sneaking a peek under my dress?"

Millie wished she had a clever comeback right then; it might've earned her points. Toots eyed her up and down.

"Well, well. Don't you look nice with your hair tied up in that ribbon! That's the one I gave you, isn't it?"

Millie twirled. "Yes, and I appreciate it sooo much!"

She hoped her delivery wasn't too over the top. Toots seemed pleased. She pointed to the manicured hedgerow. "Do you know how many different kinds of roses I have?"

"Fifteen!" Millie answered. Her mother had told her the number at least fifteen times. "Can I go to the pet shop today?"

"And do you remember their names?"

Millie sighed. She did know a few. Like the common Tea Rose, the red one most people picture when they think of a rose. Easy to remember, since the only tea her mother drank was the Red Rose brand. Then there was Blue Girl, her mother's favorite, which looked more lavender than blue. And finally, Millie's favorite: Fire and Ice. The petals were pure white with red-tinged edges, as if they were dipped in blood.

"No," Millie replied. It was the only answer her mother wanted to hear.

"Come, follow me," Toots said, waving her hand.

And so, for what felt like forever, Millie was given a tour of the garden, *again,* and told the story of each rose, *again.* There was no doubt that Toots had a remarkable green thumb. And it stuck out. Their postage-stamp lot was the talk of the town, and pretty enough to be on a stamp, too.

Millie was terribly distracted. Puffy clouds were drifting across the blue sky, forming animal shapes. Fish, bunnies, turtles... they all reminded her of one thing: she had a mission that needed a mother's permission!

"Can I go to the pet shop today?" she asked again. She'd reached the end of the tour, *and* her patience. "Patrick will be here, and—"

"Mother's Day," Toots interrupted, leaning over a low bush at the end of the row. She snipped a tiny red rose off and tucked it behind Millie's ear. "Isn't it a sweet name? Mother's Day? I ordered this bush as a gift to myself, all the way from England. You were just three."

"Uh-huh. About the pet store. We need—"

Millie reached into her pants and pulled out the fish food. She was now ready to convince her mother that the container was half empty, not half full—therefore a trip to the pet store was an emergency!

Toots glanced at her watch. "Holy smoke! Where'd the time go? Yeah, yeah, okay. I've got a man visiting today. You know what to do. Make yourself scarce then."

Patrick stood at the kitchen sink, watching birds flutter around the feeder outside. He was tall for eleven, and skinny as Gumby; everything about him seemed lengthy and stretched. He wore dungarees and a faded purple T-shirt, both of which were thin and tight.

Moving slowly, as though he had all the time in the world, he rinsed his empty plate, dried it with a towel, and returned it to the cupboard. Millie, meanwhile, buzzed with nervous energy. Unsatisfied with one sandwich, she quickly made another. She squirted ketchup on the bread, added bologna, and topped it with a fistful of potato chips before pressing it flat.

"So, what do you need at O'Brien's?" Patrick asked, growing curious about her strange behavior.

As he asked, he turned around like a graceful gazelle, his hand flipping a towel over his shoulder. Two rings glinted on his fingers. Patrick always had an elegant way about him. He crouched to pet Millie's dog.

"You poor little guy being given a name like *Lady*bug," he said, shooting Millie a playful glance. "Can he come with us? We can tie him up outside."

Millie shook her head no; her lips still attached to her sandwich. Her cousin was two years older—and her best friend—but she just wanted to get to the pet store without having to explain anything.

Although his question reminded her of something. She had painted a picture that won first place in an art class competition. Swallowing quickly, she jumped up. The picture wasn't on the fridge.

"Mother!" she hollered, leaning around the corner. "Where's that painting I did of Ladybug? I wanna show Patrick!"

"How should I know?!" Toots snapped from the bedroom.

"Oops," Millie muttered. Through the front window, she spotted a car parked outside. She had forgotten a man was coming over.

"For land's sake," Patrick said, seeing it too. "I know Leo's way older than Aunt Toots, but you'd think she'd wait until he leaves for work before having some guy over to—"

"Shush," Millie interrupted. She grabbed a long-sleeved shirt from a hook and tied it around her waist. Then she snatched a handful of coins from the milk money jar. "Both our families are fruit baskets. You know that."

Patrick burst out laughing. "What a hoot! You just blended fruitcakes and basket cases to make your own word!"

Millie chuckled in response. She often mixed sayings together—usually by accident. When someone pointed it out, she was a good sport about it. They *were* pretty funny.

As quickly as Patrick laughed, however, he turned solemn. He knew what Millie had said—or meant to say—was true.

"Let's go," Millie said. She held the door open for Patrick, noticing a shadow of sadness over his eyes. For a split second she wondered if he too had been... but she stopped herself.

*No, I can't think about sad things right now,* she thought, following him outside. *I must stay focused!*

Millie walked beside Patrick. The sky was a cheerful blue, and the clouds were still forming animal shapes. It felt like the perfect time to discuss her plans for living on a farm in the country with him. They'd have chickens, a cow, and not just one horse... but one in every color.

"It's going to be so wonderful, you know it, Patrick?"

Patrick shrugged, kicking at the air with his sneakers. He liked dreaming with Millie, and he also knew she wanted to marry him someday. It's just that his mind was tormented with confusing thoughts lately. Talking to Millie about them didn't seem right. She already had a heap of her own craziness to sort out.

At the entrance of O'Brien's, Patrick gave a ready signal.

"One, two, three!" they counted in unison, then burst through the glass door together.

The first thing they felt was a blast of hot, humid air, making sweat bead on their faces. This was quickly followed by the nose-piercing scent of animal fur, fish tanks, and wet hay.

They tilted their glistening faces until they heard a bird squawk.

"Ha! I was right!" Patrick gloated.

Earlier at lunch, each of them had guessed what sound they would hear the moment they walked through the door. Millie had bet on Patch, the one-eyed kitten turned cat. The poor thing seemed born with a meower on repeat.

Patrick had chosen Wendel, the Scarlet Macaw. He remembered that Mr. O'Brien chained the bird's foot to a cageless perch for exactly two hours every afternoon. Handsome and mouthy, Wendel was quite a schmoozer. There wasn't a customer he couldn't charm into buying him penny peanuts from his snack dispenser.

Millie glanced around nervously. Mr. O'Brien was behind the counter, unpacking boxes. He was short and balding, with bulging muscles and a handlebar mustache. Someone in Millie's class said that he used to be in the circus—either as trapeze artist or an elephant trainer—and had gotten some of his animals from there. Millie didn't know if she believed all that. But Mr. O'Brien *was* odd, and he spoke with a lisp. Millie once described the sound to Patrick as "having a cabbage in his mouth."

"Do something for me," Millie whispered. She pulled some coins from her pocket and held them out. "Buy the cheapest can of fish food for me. If you need more time, talk to Mr. O'Brien. Pretend you're interested in Lily."

Lily was a Pygmy Marmoset monkey that Millie wished on a thousand stars she could own. Small enough to sleep in a teacup, she had the adorable habit of walking upright while carrying armfuls of food.

But Lily was getting old—likely because no one could afford Mr. O'Brien's asking price. Or maybe he just didn't want to sell her. Whenever anyone showed interest, he'd wave them off saying, "Lily is high maintenance... worse than my wife!"

Patrick took the coins and hesitated.

"Go on," Millie urged. "Don't let hair grow under your feet!"

*Hair? Feet?* Patrick rolled his eyes and shuffled toward the fish aisle.

With her accomplice on distraction duty, Millie hurried to the back of the store and stopped at an aquarium. It was a low tank, with an open top and sides that were short enough for her to reach inside.

"Don't worry, mama," she whispered to a painted turtle resting in a pool of shallow water. She wiped black mold off a piece of lettuce in the tank and held it up to her nose. "Here, try to eat. Your babies will be okay."

While Millie was talking to turtles, Patrick paid for the fish food and started getting impatient. Mr. O'Brien was as well. He returned to his boxes, clearly uninterested in answering any more questions about exotic monkeys from a skinny boy whose tight jeans showed no evidence of extra money in his pockets, let alone the kind of money *his* monkey cost.

To Patrick's relief, Millie finally appeared, rushing around the corner. She was walking funny, arms stiff at her sides as if they wouldn't bend. With just her eyes and a jerk of her head, she signaled him to open the door.

Once outside and out of sight, Patrick exploded. "What the blazes is wrong with your arms?!"

"Follow me!" Millie said, waddling like a penguin down an alley toward the part of the canal where the water was low and murky. She paced back and forth until she seemed satisfied. "Quick, unsnap my sleeves!"

After Patrick did so, Millie shook her arms, sending baby turtles flying out. *Five dollars'* worth of turtles to be exact! Each fifty-cent piece plopped into the water one by one.

"What the hell?" Patrick shouted, exasperated. "What's the matter with you?"

"Stop shouting at me!" she hollered back. "They weren't happy! The lettuce was moldy, and the water bowl poopy. I promised Mama Turtle last week I would help her babies."

Patrick looked down at the ten tiny turtles, their limbs stretched out paddling through the water with complete abandon. The little guys *did* look happy.

"Talk about coming out of a shell," he laughed. "Still, Millie, come on. That was a crazy stunt. Mr. O'Brien's going to know it was you. He's never liked you, you know."

"I'll be fine," Millie said, rubbing her arms to make sure there weren't any more turtles up her sleeves.

"No, you won't be fine. You're going to get in trouble, I tell you. You remember what happened to Dennis when he stole those candy cigarettes?"

Patrick then went on with a long, detailed story about his brother that lasted the entire walk home. Millie barely listened. Her cousin loved to talk, and he had an amazing memory. He could recall names, dates, random events—he could probably talk the wings off a fly!

Nothing he said made Millie worry. After all, this wasn't her first time stealing. When she was about four years old, her mother once pushed her in a cart at Woolworths department store when they had passed a display of rings. Toots picked out a silvery- blue one and slipped it into Millie's palm. "Keep your fist tight," she whispered. "If you keep it closed until we get to the car, I'll buy you an ice cream cone!"

And so, Millie had kept her fist closed, and her mother had opened hers—at the counter of Carvel's dairy bar. Needless to say, it was a naughtily happy memory: she and her mother squeezed together on the outside bench licking their Pink Marshmallow soft-serves with Toots wearing the shiny ring and a proud smile on her face.

"Are you even listening to me?" Patrick asked, noticing Millie's mind was elsewhere. Suddenly, he stopped. "Uh-oh, I told you. O'Brien called her."

Millie followed Patrick's finger. Toots was standing next to her car, hands on her hips. The passenger door was open.

"Get in!" she said to Millie when she arrived. "Right now! Patrick, go in the house. Your mother will be here shortly."

Millie slipped into the car and was scolded all the way to the pet shop, then found herself standing in front of the circus man who now reminded her of Popeye. Frustrated, she kicked the bottom edge of the counter.

"I'm sorry. I won't do it again," she mumbled, repeating what she'd been told to say.

*Right? Wrong? Why was it all so confusing?*

Toots hoisted her handbag onto the counter and asked Mr. O'Brien what was owed. When he answered five dollars, she sucked in air.

"That's highway robbery!" she yelled, loud enough for the customers in the store to hear. "Give me a bulk price."

After finally getting her way, Toots pulled out four one-dollar bills and lined them up on the counter. She had several rings on her fingers, and incidentally, one of them was the silvery-blue Woolworths ring!

Millie then had a crazy thought. Maybe her mother would stop for Carvel's ice cream on the way home!

# CHAPTER 4

# The Old Rugged Cross

G eorge Bernard Shaw once said, "You don't stop laughing when you grow old; you grow old when you stop laughing."

If Shaw was right, then the year Millie turned twelve, she was older than old. Her body was starting to change, and not in ways she wanted. She had stained someone's patio cushion with her first period. She was fighting with her mother a lot. And she couldn't remember the last time she laughed.

Being a pre-teen is an awkward time on life's clock... like being stuck between a tick and a tock. Half the time Millie wasn't sure who she was. The other half, she didn't *like* who she was. Something about her life felt "off." Was it her? Or the world?

One humid August day, her mood was especially sour. They were getting ready to leave for Aunt Mabel's, where her cousin Gail was having a potluck-style wedding reception. Toots and Leo were packing the car, hurrying to not be late.

Millie wasn't helping; she was simmering. Her mother had recently rearranged the attic and had either taken or lost some of Millie's things.

One of the missing items was the little button the old woman with the funny hat had given her years ago in church. Millie kept it on her vanity and looked at it often. She didn't yet know what she believed about God, but she did pray to him sometimes. She wanted to believe he loved her—that she wasn't "junk." *But sometimes...*

Millie stood with folded arms outside the car door, glaring at Toots who was loading a casserole through the back hatch. Leo quietly waited behind her, holding lawn chairs.

"Where is it?" Millie demanded. "The button that was on my vanity? And the gemstone I found at the state fair? I can't find either one."

Toots's face was dripping with sweat. Her expression shifted from agitation to disgust. Her once-sweet, angelic daughter was starting to act ugly and devilish.

"What? Blast it, Millie. You already asked me; I told you I don't know, and you know perfectly well I cleaned the vanity to make room for your jewelry box. You're such an ingrate!"

Millie huffed and Toots pointed at her. "You better get in the car right now or I'll slap your mouth."

*I'll slap you back,* Millie muttered under her breath. She slid into the back seat and slammed the door.

She knew, of course, that she wouldn't slap her mother. Toots was too strong. The very air Millie breathed was her mother's breath. Was there no escaping its intensity? No way to avoid spinning helplessly in its hurricane-like force?

Millie rubbed her hands together and looked at her wrists, feeling the urge to scratch them.

Fortunately, Ladybug was in the back seat with her. He nuzzled Millie, pushing his head beneath her hand.

Millie scratched his favorite spot, the one under his flea collar, prompting a series of happy grunts.

Other than that, the ride was quiet. Aunt Mabel's house, near

Lake Ontario, was about thirty minutes northeast of Rochester. As they got closer, the sky darkened, and Millie noticed the birds flying low.

*I wish I could fly,* she thought. *Fly away from my mother!*

The moment they turned into Aunt Mabel's driveway, Toots and Millie put their spat behind them. More relatives than Millie had ever seen in one place milled around outside, filling the garage and spilling out onto the front lawn. Even Toots's two out-of-state brothers, Richard and Lloyd, were there with their kids.

For a while everything went smoothly, until the sky rumbled and the women had to scramble to bring the food inside. Most of the older kids were already there, crammed into the living room watching TV or playing board games.

Millie tried to stay close to Patrick, even though her cousin was almost fifteen now, with his own life. She also had found out that he was attracted to boys, so marrying him was a childish dream she had to bury.

Meanwhile, Ladybug, who got nervous during storms, followed Millie everywhere. She tried to shake him. She ran from room to room giggling whenever he sniffed her out... although he might have been after her hotdogs! Millie was eating a lot of them that day. She kept skipping between the living room and the kitchen, then back again, playfully carrying another hotdog and soda in her hands. Her mother laughed at her antics, and for some reason, Millie thought everyone else was laughing too.

"Geez, is that girl going to leave any for my kids?" Uncle Richard said when Millie got another hotdog. This time it was her favorite: a white hot—a pale but tasty Rochester variation. "Maybe we need to put a limit on them."

A few others snickered at his comment.

Toots bore her steely-gray eyes into her brother. Then she cursed at him.

"You're a communist!" she snarled.

The tension thickened, and Millie froze in place like a weird statue holding a mustard bottle over a bun. The sudden awareness that the uproar was about *her* was mortifying!

"She's spoiled, Aunt Toots. That's all he's saying," Gail chimed in. "She gets what she wants, whenever she wants, and you—"

Toots shot up, knocking over her chair. Her eyes narrowed, and her lips puffed out. She jabbed a finger at her niece's chest.

"That's all he's saying, huh? Or is that all *you're* saying?"

Millie quickly ran outside. In the side yard stood a rusty metal swing set. She squeezed into a swing too small for her body and took a big, angry bite out of her hotdog. Ladybug moseyed up, sat down, and whined.

"Go away!" she yelled—but at the same time, threw him the rest of her hotdog. Suddenly, she felt a fullness she didn't experience very often.

Twisting in the swing, she felt its chains wrap around her like a hungry python.

*I always eat too much!* she thought, groaning. *Why do I keep doing it?*

Maybe it was because eating was the only time when everything felt right in her world. She never felt lonely lying on her belly watching an episode of *Lassie,* scarfing down mashed potatoes and pan-fried chicken. Anger, shame, sadness—none of it existed with a mouthful of pasta, pizza, or hotdogs.

Or maybe she ate so much because her mother encouraged it. Toots always seemed pleased when Millie accepted her "offerings," as if Millie was a god and food was her appeasement.

*Uh-oh!* Sprinkles dotted her bare arms. *Think, think. Where should I go if it rains?*

Inside wasn't an option—loud voices still spilled from the windows. The garage? She thought better of that, too; *he* was there.

And although the car felt safer, it was parked near the garage where *he* might see her.

This "he" person was a close relative of Millie's. For a long time, she had trouble saying his name—that is, until she learned to avoid him. Before that, starting when she was around six or seven, he would take her into his basement. She knew she should have told somebody what he was doing, but she figured everyone already knew, and just didn't care. Often, when he inappropriately touched a woman or made a suggestive comment, people would excuse it with remarks like, "It's just the way he is," or "He's a skirt-chaser."

In fact, Millie had grown up thinking lewdness and vulgarity were normal family behaviors. She'd even started acting that way herself—which, sadly, led full circle back to food.

"Hey, Mil'!"

Millie stopped twisting in the swing and straightened up. It was her cousin, Jimmy.

"Hey," he repeated, leaning out from behind the house. "C'mere. You gotta see this!"

Millie dug her toes into the sand. She wasn't in a hurry. She disliked Jimmy almost as much as the man whose name she didn't want to say—and for similar reasons.

"Come on, Bow-Legger!" came another voice from the back-yard. It was Dennis, the oldest of the cousins. "You *really* need to see this!"

Millie was confused that Dennis kept calling her that. Plus, a few years previous, another cousin (she was told it was Gail) had put a note in her jacket pocket that read, *"Millie has bowed legs—just like her mother—and they're going to split apart."*

As horrifying as that sounded, neither she nor Toots had bowed legs—at least not that Millie could tell. She had even asked Aunt Mabel what it meant, but her aunt nervously changed the subject.

Eventually, Millie chalked it up to a common insult, like "Your mother wears army boots."

More scuffling and guffawing came from the boys. Millie jumped off the swing and slipped into her sandals. "Alright, alright, I'm coming."

"Hurry up," Dennis said to Jimmy. "She's coming. Squirt the blood on me."

Jimmy, who worshiped the air his older brother breathed, practically tripped over himself to grab the ketchup bottle.

"On my head, dufus," Dennis said, snatching the bottle from his hands and doing it himself.

When Millie rounded the bend, her mouth dropped open. Somehow, using only rusty handsaws, rope, and scavenged pieces of old lumber, the two teenage boys had managed to build a full-sized cross in the backyard!

The impressive structure rose from a mound of dirt and attached to the top of the vertical post was a sign that read: "King of the Jews,"—with the letters "w" and "s" squashed at the end to make them fit.

At the bottom of the cross sat a plastic milk crate. Dennis, ridiculously smeared with Heinz ketchup, stepped on it and reached for the horizontal beam of the cross. Then, slowly, trying not to lose his balance, he turned around to face forward.

"I am dying for you, Millie!" he bellowed, stretching out his arms and throwing his head back with theatrical agony. "I am dying for you, and your many, ma-a-a-ny sins!"

Below the cross, Jimmy roared with laughter.

Millie crossed her arms and frowned. She had plenty of opinions and was forming new ones every day. And although she didn't know what she thought of Jesus—whether he was God's son and had "risen from the dead," as her Aunt Ethel wrote in her Easter cards—she knew one thing for sure. Jesus was at least a *somebody,* and a somebody's death shouldn't be mocked by *anybody.*

"That's not funny," she said. "You both are knuckleheads."

Dennis, fueled by her reaction, threw his head back again.

"Millie Saxe is a bastard girl," he shouted. "And she needs her many sins washed away!"

Millie's face flushed with anger. "Bastard" was another name the boys called her—sometimes attached to absurd lies. Or were they? Lately, Millie couldn't tell. Nothing in her life was feeling certain.

She turned around to leave.

"Bastard blood for bastard blood!" Jimmy jeered behind her. Then he looked up to see if his idol on the cross approved of his wisecrack.

Millie spun around and stormed toward Jimmy. Up close, she could smell the nauseating odor of corn chips on his breath.

"I am not a bastard!" she screamed in his face.

Jimmy stepped back, eyes wide. He had four years on Millie, but not as many inches. He looked to Dennis and tittered. "Gee whiz, calm down, maniac. We're just having fun."

Millie raised a hand to cut him off.

"Don't talk to me," she said sharply, then marched toward the front yard.

By now, daylight had dimmed, and the trees were thrashing in the wind. Not wanting to get caught in the storm, Millie picked up her pace.

When she rounded the corner, she ran into a different kind of storm. Toots was marching down the walkway with Leo trailing behind her carrying chairs and Tupperware containers.

"You can all go to hell!" Toots shouted, making the people standing near her car jump back. "My family is dead to me!"

Knowing Toots would call for her soon, Millie backed up and ducked around the corner. Her heart pounded as she pressed her back against the house. She felt trapped. The backyard—where she'd just come from—had left her shaken with anger and confusion. But the front yard—where she was headed—promised more of the same.

The only place that felt remotely safe was the cross. She had a sudden urge to run back to it for reasons she didn't fully understand. Was it to say a quick prayer, believing the foot of a cross was the best place for that? Or was it a strange need to confirm the monstrosity still stood... that she hadn't simply imagined it?

Whatever the reason, Millie broke from her frozen stance and dashed back.

*Real quick,* she told herself, *I'll be back in a second.*

The funny thing about personal experiences, is how flighty they can be. Years later, the memory might be lost, or its details faded and muddled. That's why what matters most is how someone *feels* about an experience.

Millie's memory of this day could have easily been marked by the bad things: anger over her lost button, the humiliation of eating too many hotdogs, the pain of being bullied. Years later, this might have been all she remembered. But when she acted on her impulse and ran back to the cross, a better story was written.

By then, her cousins had dashed for shelter. The cross stood alone at the edge of the hayfield. Against the ominous sky, it almost looked like a lighthouse; its dull gray wood transformed into a glowing beacon.

Millie gasped when she saw it. Electricity lit up the sky, and seagulls, gliding in and out of silver-edged clouds, hovered above the cross like feathery angels.

Of course, what she was really looking at was just a ridiculous, ketchup-stained mockery built by two irreligious teenage boys. Standing closer now, she could see how poorly constructed it was. There was no way it would survive the night.

Still, the sight of it standing alone in the looming storm was strangely moving. It made her want to weep. She thought of her cousins' taunts. *Jesus died for my sins? What does that even mean?*

There was no time to linger. A flash of lightning split the sky, followed by a deafening crack over the field. Rain began to fall.

Millie sprinted to the car, jumped in, and slammed the door... making it just in time.

Toots and Leo had already loaded the car, including Ladybug, and the engine was running. The moment Leo pulled onto the road, the sky cracked open and unleashed sheets of blinding rain. He gripped the steering wheel, squinting through the frantic wipers. Beside him, Toots sobbed and cursed the day her sister and her kids were born—even threatening to end her own life.

Millie patted the seat next to her, signaling for Ladybug to come closer. Trembling, he crawled onto her chest, muddy paws and all. Millie was a mess herself; her clothes damp, her sandals caked with wet grass.

She wrapped a large, dry towel around them both. Then she closed her eyes and leaned her head against the window.

Behind her eyelids, an eerie glow-in-the-dark outline of the cross lingered.

"Shh," she whispered to Ladybug, who was nuzzling his nose into her neck. "Go to sleep now. We're okay."

# CHAPTER 5

# Opening a Pandora's Box

Leaning wearily on a card table, Millie held up a blue puzzle piece and squinted at the picture on the box. *Did it go in the ocean—or the sky?*

Outside, a bitter wind howled. Inside, a record player howled too, playing a melancholy Patsy Cline album Millie didn't like. It reminded her how much she missed Aunt Mabel and Patrick. Even though two years had passed since the infamous "hotdog caper," Toots still held a grudge and refused to speak to any of them.

Finally! The piece, tinged with a bit of white, found its place in a frothy wave. Millie almost didn't want to pick up another one.

"Why do they make puzzles with such boring scenes?" she grumbled.

It wasn't that Millie didn't love beaches; they were, in fact, her "happy place." She could spend hours playing in the warm sand, collecting shells, and floating in the water (a buoyant perk of being overweight) without a single negative thought. She even loved puzzles for a similar reason: they let her escape.

But this puzzle wasn't that. The only interesting parts—if you could call them that—were a ship on the horizon, two seagulls in the sky, and calligraphy at the bottom which read:

*"You, O God, are the hope of everyone on earth, even those who sail on distant seas. Psalm 12:5."*

Millie ran her hand along the verse, the section she'd finished first. The smoothness felt comforting, even though the puzzle wasn't complete. So many troubling thoughts were scattered in her fourteen-year-old head, like a puzzle without a box lid. She needed hope. She needed the chaotic, fragmented pieces of her life to come together into a smooth, cohesive picture.

Could God do that? She wasn't sure. Sometimes she prayed to him. She prayed to a God she didn't know, asking him for answers to questions she couldn't articulate. She even entertained the idea of being an alien born through a human mother. That would make Jimmy right. She *would* be a bastard, then.

Crackling static came from the record player. Millie got up, swapped the record, and pulled on another sweater. A glance out the window showed little change. The snowplows were only able to clear a single lane, piling the rest of the snow on top of the cars parked along the street.

She sat down to take another stab at the puzzle. What else was there to do? It was the second day since a "Nor'easter" struck the Great Lakes region, dumping heavy snowfall and knocking out power across the area. All the schools in Rochester were closed, and most businesses too.

The storm hadn't caught the Saxes unprepared, though. As soon as the warnings had come, Toots—excitable about storms—gathered oil lamps, candles, and filled the bathtub and every container she could find with water. And Leo—who'd forgotten to remove the screen in the attic—came upstairs to replace it with a storm window.

After the worst of the snow had fallen, their neighbor Trudy trudged through the drifts to check on them and bring the boring beach puzzle.

"To get you excited for your Florida vacation," she had said, winking through her horn-rimmed glasses when she handed Millie the box.

It was a nice gesture, Millie supposed; Trudy was a thoughtful neighbor—the same woman who had given her the hermit crabs. Still, Millie wasn't thrilled about the announcement Toots had made to Trudy and everyone else that they'd be going to Florida after school let out. A ten-day road trip, just the two of them...

"Excited" was the *last* thing Millie felt.

Still, she was glad they'd be staying with Aunt Ethel in Florida, who was Toots's aunt. She wasn't local family, but family none-theless.

Leaving the puzzle half-finished, Millie got up from the table to find something else to do. Maybe a craft of some kind? She glanced at the far end of the attic where the storage room was located, hesitating to move in that direction. Even though it stored things like craft supplies and games, she *hated* the room. It was a cramped, dark, and had a musty smell. And it certainly didn't help that she read a book once about a little boy who was locked in a room just like it. Nobody had known he was there for years, except for his mentally disabled sister who fed him bread and cheese under the door.

*Com'on, get a grip,* Millie scolded herself, taking a deep breath. *I'm fourteen—not some scaredy-cat kid.*

Lest she wake Toots from her nap, Millie carefully tiptoed past the stairwell to the storage room door. Then she lifted the latch and stepped in.

It took a moment for her eyes to adjust. The bright sun reflecting off the snow outside was the room's only light, streaming in through a small window. It transformed the specks of dust in the air into tiny floating crystals.

"What a mess," she muttered, looking around. Through the haze she could see old hat boxes, dusty board games, and stacks of twine-bundled newspapers. A silver tinsel-tree stood in the corner, still decorated, as well as several plastic nativity statues for the yard —including baby Jesus who haplessly lay upside down on the floor.

Then there was the Black Santa. It stood like a sentry in the room, staring straight ahead with its large, marble-white eyes. Millie was horrified when Toots had first purchased the five-foot figurine and tied it to a flagpole in their front yard. Rochester was under the strain of racial tensions; an issue that was worsening every day. Toots had meant the display as a show of solidarity, but Millie was teased at school because of it... by both white *and* black kids who saw it.

Millie's breath quickened and faint clouds formed in the crisp, unheated air. Just thinking about the Santa chagrin made her feel claustrophobic. Whether it was at home, school, or right in her own front yard, trouble seemed to find her and suffocate her.

Off to the side of Santa, Millie noticed a colorful box wrapped in shiny paper. It sat askew on a high shelf, but the label on the front was visible. It read, "Toots/Private."

*A box of secrets?* Millie's chest fluttered. It was almost impossible to get Toots to talk about her past. Maybe the contents of the box would finally reveal why? Millie also read another book—a less scary one—about a girl named Nancy Drew. Nancy had found a box once too, and the clues inside helped her find a missing person!

Still, Millie knew snooping was wrong. She slowly rubbed the back of her neck, wondering if she should give in to her curiosity.

*I guess it's just my woman's intuition. Every woman has one, you know.*

Millie squared her shoulders, amazed at how she had recalled these words by Nancy Drew at such a perfect moment!

*Yes, I'm a woman. I have intuition,* she repeated to herself as she walked over to the shelf. She slid a crate in front of the shelves, climbed on top, and carefully pulled down the box. After setting it on the floor and lifting the lid, she muttered a curse.

*Paperwork.* Millie *hated* paperwork. She gave the papers a quick stir to see if there was something underneath. That's when her eyes landed on a curious manila envelope labeled: *Adoption Application.*

She opened it with shaky hands. *Adopted?* That could explain a lot! But the document inside was an application Toots had submitted about a year before Millie was born. The front page was stamped in red: *REJECTED.*

*Too bad,* Millie thought. *It would've been nice to have a brother or sister!*

With curiosity now piqued, Millie started pulling papers out of the box.

Boring. Put back. Boring. Put back. Interesting. Keep...

Nancy would've been proud. Millie sorted the papers like a seasoned sleuth. Anything with big words like "loans," "liens," or "property deeds" went back into the box, while cards and hand-written letters stayed in her lap.

She even made quick work of those.

There was a particular notecard, however, that Millie lingered over. It was postmarked from California eleven months after Millie was born, and inside the card was a photo of a woman in a bikini. The note read:

*Dear Toots,*

*Ted finished my sunroom yesterday. I love it.*

*So much light comes in. I wish you could help me with the flower garden. Or paint the town like we used to (Ha ha). I know, we are big girls now. Adults, can you believe it? And you are busy with baby Mildred. I'm glad to hear you have her now. That bow-legged brat didn't deserve her. Be well. Come visit someday, okay?*

> *Your ol' bestie,*
> *Sandra*

Millie rubbed her forehead. *Have her now? Bow-legged brat?* She recalled how her cousins used to tease her, saying she had bowed legs "like her mother's." She also remembered how nervous Aunt Mabel had acted when Millie asked her about it.

*Could it be?* Millie wondered, goosebumps rising on her arms. *Could this bow-legged woman be my mother, and not Toots?*

The sound of a flapping shingle outside the window startled her. It was getting late; Toots would be making dinner soon.

As quickly as she could, Millie threw everything back into the box, returned it to the shelf, and slipped out of the room.

*Now what?* She hesitated, pausing with her hand on the latch. She felt dizzy with all the swirling questions in her head.

Who was this woman Toots had taken in? If she was adopted, why weren't there any official papers? And if Leo wasn't her real father, then who was?

And even more unsettling... If Toots wasn't her real mother, why had she told everyone she gave birth to her? *Why all the lies?*

There were only two things Millie was certain of. She had just opened a Pandora's box, and somehow, she *had* to find answers.

# CHAPTER 6

# The Search for a Sign

P atrick dropped his playing cards on the grass, stretched his arms behind his head, and yawned.

"You sure you want to play again?" he asked Millie, looking at his watch. "It's getting late."

Beside him sat Nellie, a plump girl with panty-hosed legs folded in a pretzel. She wrinkled her freckled nose as she rifled through her purse for a cigarette.

Between the three teens, the smell of Marlboros, hot cocoa, and lilacs mingled in the crisp spring air.

Millie gathered the cards and gave them a shuffle, stealing a glance at Patrick. It was good to see her cousin again. At seventeen, he seemed more mature, his once-skinny features now subtly filled out. Millie had recently called him collect from a school phone to tell him about the note she'd found in the attic. That's when he said he had a new set of wheels and could meet her and her friend Nellie at Lilac Park.

Toots, of course, didn't know any of this.

"Yes, I agree," Nellie said, siding with Patrick. She lit her cigarette, took a drag, then exhaled a long, slow puff. "I'm worried what your mother will do if you come home late. Remember when we skipped school and took the tram downtown? What a snafu!"

Millie, a cigarette dangling unlit from her mouth, shook her head and dealt another round. Nellie meant well, and yes, Toots *had* been upset. She nearly put Millie's face on a milk carton!

It just wasn't a concern for Millie anymore, having learned over time how to better manage her mother's moods. One of her most effective tricks was to simply be home by eight o'clock in the evening. If she was on the couch by then, watching *Matlock* and eating leftovers, Toots didn't care what her daughter had done all day. She never even asked.

Nellie leaned back against a tree and sighed. "Well, I'm done playing."

She held out a lighter to Millie. "Here. Are you gonna smoke that thing or just gum it to death?"

Millie smirked and snatched the lighter.

Nellie, also fifteen, was in the same grade as Millie. She had short, choppy auburn hair that was always styled by the wind, a contagiously throaty laugh, and shared with Millie a strong dislike for both school *and* home.

They were a match made in heaven for after-school adventures. Walking home from school—on the spotty days they went—was rarely complete without daring each other into mischief. This included everything from stealing candy at the 5 & Dime store, to breaking into the abandoned theatre on Webster Avenue and dancing on its rickety stage in front of an invisible audience.

Having heard some of their stories earlier, Patrick had said the two of them would "spell trouble with a capital T" if they weren't so good at not getting caught.

"I'm done, too," Patrick said, chuckling. "I'm tired of losing."

"Whatever," Millie said, rolling onto her side. She rested her head on her hand and gazed across the landscape of Rochester's iconic park. Everywhere she looked, bushes dotted the hilly, winding paths, bursting with fluffy buds in shades of lavender, purple, and white. It was a fragrant display of the park's charm, and a sign its annual Lilac Festival was near.

But Millie wasn't enjoying the view. She was sulking. During the card game she had *again* told Patrick and Nellie about the suspicious note in the attic, but they didn't say much. She really wanted feedback.

"So, guys," she tried again, "don't you have any thoughts about what I told you earlier? I just *know* something is fishy in Denmark!"

Patrick laughed. "Rotten, Millie. Rotten."

"It's not rotten," she snapped. "It's serious."

Nellie threw her hands up in the air, laughing. "I'm out of this!"

Patrick squinted and pursed his lips, trying to look serious. Unamused, Millie flicked her cigarette butt at his leg. He swatted it away.

"Geez, Millie," he said, dusting the ashes off his pants. "I already told you; I agree that Aunt Toots isn't your real mother. I've always thought that."

"Why? What made you think that?"

"I don't know, I guess as long as I can remember us kids overheard things—things that hinted there might be a skeleton in your closet. I also heard that funny thing about your mother having bowed legs, which didn't make sense to me, either. But you know how Toots was—always hell-bent on convincing everyone she gave birth to you. It was hard to know anything for sure."

A sober silence hung in the air. Patrick continued.

"But it was never a big deal to me. You've always been my favorite cousin."

Millie rolled her eyes.

Nellie looked thoughtful, then asked Millie, "Does your mother know about your suspicions? Have you asked her about any of this?"

Millie sat up. *Finally,* someone was engaging.

"Yes," she said, "I mean, yes, I tried to talk to her. But it didn't go well. After I saw the card in the attic, I asked her what causes bowleggedness, and if a child can inherit it from a mother. I figured that might open the door to asking if I was adopted."

"What did she say to *that?"* Nellie asked, wide-eyed. Her round face, which tended to flush, was lit up with curiosity.

"Nothing, at first. She just stood there like a cat bit her tongue."

"Ouch!" Patrick interjected, unable to help himself.

Millie ignored him and continued speaking to Nellie. "Then she got weird, you know? Like, crazy weird. She pulled out my baby album and made me look through it, saying things like, 'You ungrateful brat. Look at that picture. And that one. You're *my* daughter, you hear? *Mine!'* She freaked out all night and wouldn't even answer my question."

"Wow," Nellie whispered. "So, you didn't tell her about finding the card in the attic?"

"No way, she would've totally snapped. But she did ask why I was asking. I just told her that when I was little, I had found a note in my pocket saying I had bowlegs. I mean, I'm still curious about that. Is it passed through birth? My legs seem normal now, but could it happen when I'm older?"

Nellie laughed. "I don't know, but it would be great for riding rodeo barrels!"

"Hey, aren't you going on a trip soon?" Patrick asked Millie. "To visit Aunt Ethel and Uncle Harvey?"

"What does that have to do with anything?"

"Oh, nothing. I just think it'll be a nice diversion for you."

Millie angrily grabbed her book bag and stood up. "I'm leaving."

"Hold it," Patrick said, standing up. He his arms around Millie. "I'm sorry. Don't worry. Everything'll be okay."

Nellie was right behind him to offer another hug. Neither one liked seeing the wrath of Millie come out.

Then Nellie took Millie's arm. "Adios, Patrick. I'm walking home with her."

On the way, Nellie tried to cheer her up.

"Patrick's right, you know. This trip might be good for you. It's Florida, for goodness' sake. I love the ocean, don't you?"

Millie shrugged. She'd been to the Jersey shore a couple of times, and the beach *was* a magical place. But she and Toots weren't exactly besties.

"Did I tell you we're stopping in D.C. for a few days to see historical sites? And my mom wants me to read maps while she drives? Yeah, that'll go great. I'm gonna be a banana case!"

"Sounds awful," Nellie giggled. Then she pointed to a sign ahead. "Ooh, look! Cream-Licks are on special. Let's stop and get one."

Millie lifted her eyes and saw a *sign*...but not the kind with a cow peeking out of an ice cream cone that Nellie saw. No, it was the phone booth next to it.

Suddenly, she knew exactly what she had to do.

"Order me the strawberry one," she said, pulling some coins from her pocket. She handed Nellie three quarters. "I'll join you in a minute."

Millie squeezed into the phone booth and dropped a dime into the slot. The operator made the connection.

"Hello? Aunt Mabel? This is Millie, your niece."

A crackling sound muffled her aunt's reply, but Millie pressed on.

"I'm calling about my mother. I think I might be adopted, but she won't tell me anything. I tried asking, but she got mad. Do *you* know anything?"

Silence. Millie pressed the receiver tightly to her ear. Then she heard her aunt say something but couldn't make it out.

"I'm sorry, Aunt Mabel, we're having a bad connection. Can you call me back at this number? I'll wait."

Through more static she caught Aunt Ethel's name, and something about the Florida trip.

"Yes, yes, we're going this summer. Leo has to work. What about Aunt Ethel?"

This time, she held the phone away from her ear. It helped.

"Talk to Ethel," she heard Aunt Mabel say. "Ask Ethel your questions and see what she says first."

Millie hung up the phone feeling excited. She rushed back to Nellie, who was already seated in a booth with a Cream-Lick bowl on each side of the table—one strawberry, one chocolate—topped with a pointy, upside-down cone. And balanced on the cone's tip was a single cherry held in place by a dollop of whipped cream.

It was enough to make two teenage girls giggle.

Millie slid into the booth.

"Do you believe in God?" she asked.

Nellie could only roll her eyes. Her mouth was already busy.

"Never mind. Just pray for me, will you? I think my Aunt Ethel in Florida knows something!"

# CHAPTER 7

# Aunt Ethel

The Georgia interstate stretched for miles, its asphalt shimmering in the summer heat. Millie poked a straw around the bottom of her McDonald's cup, then tossed it onto the floor behind her seat.

"I'm so glad the air conditioning is working again!" she said, leaning back.

Toots nodded heartily. When the vents started blowing hot air in Virginia, she had completely lost her cool. She paid big bucks in New York for that feature—a *working* feature—but blamed the first Ford mechanic along the route for its failure. The man had wisely chosen to work overtime to avoid the fury of a large, angry woman.

Millie reclined her seat and fluffed the pillow under her head. The warm sunlight through the side window made for a pleasant contrast to the cold air chilling her skin.

TGIS: *Thank God It's Summer.* Millie coined the acronym herself—or she thought she had. Even though she'd skipped a lot of school that year, it still seemed to drag on. Mean girls, boring classes... *gym class.* It all had made her want to tear her hair out.

Science was the one exception. Mr. Brown, her teacher, believed

Mother Nature left clues for anyone curious enough to look for them—and he had a funny way of making his point.

"What's the question we want to ask next?" he'd challenge the class, promising to do a jig for anyone who followed his line of reasoning. Millie didn't consider herself to be brainy, but the first time she made Mr. Brown dance she had almost thought otherwise!

Pulling a book out of the car's side pocket, Millie held it warily between two pinched fingers. *The World of Spiders.* Mr. Brown had given it to her on the last day of school. "Make friends with your enemy," he whispered to her, knowing she was *deathly* afraid of spiders. The way he had said it made her feel like she was being sent on a dangerous adventure!

She glanced sideways at her mother. Toots gripped the wheel tightly, but her face was as relaxed as the light morning traffic.

With a shudder she put the spider book back. It wasn't time for creepy-crawlies. The closer they got to Florida, the more her nerves frayed. *What kind of sleuthing awaited her at Aunt Ethel's? Would she uncover something shocking? Hurtful? Would she even get a chance to speak to her aunt alone?*

She shifted in her seat. Toots looked over and broke into song.

"Row, row, row your boat, gently down the *ocean...?*" She paused, waiting.

Millie giggled and finished. "Merrily, merrily, merrily, merrily, life is but a... *potion?*"

A smile danced across Toots's face, and just then, Millie wished she could gather these rare, warm-hearted moments with Toots and save them for a colder day.

She unfolded a map and spread it across her lap.

"So, it looks like we'll be on this highway for..." Millie paused, tracing the route. She felt clever for marking a ten-mile span on her fingernail with a ballpoint pen. After counting under her breath, she straightened up.

"Sixty miles!" she announced.

Maybe she shouldn't have sounded so sure; reading maps wasn't exactly her strong suit. On the trip down, they'd gotten hopelessly lost in D.C., spending hours driving in circles, arguing, and barely seeing any landmarks.

Toots fidgeted and stretched her neck. "My back is killing me. I hope they have a comfortable bed."

"Does Aunt Ethel know we're arriving tonight?"

"Mm-hm," Toots replied. "That woman better not get on my nerves or I'm booking a hotel."

Millie gulped. *That would ruin everything!*

Then again, she was surprised Toots hadn't gotten a hotel to begin with. Ethel was a sassy woman with strong opinions, and an arsenal of Bible verses to back them up. She and Harvey had lived in Rochester when Millie was younger, and Millie remembered Toots and Ethel once going at it like alley cats while Harvey watched from his chair—a beer in one hand and a cigar in the other—like he was enjoying a sporting event.

Millie took a deep breath. She was probably about to stir up a hornet's nest.

"Does Aunt Ethel have family photos? Like when you were little? Or of your mother?"

Toots shot her a wary look. "I don't know. Why?"

Millie shrugged, trying to sound casual. "Just curious. I haven't seen many photos of you as a kid, except that one where you're on a street corner with Aunt Mabel. Where were you going, by the way? You looked like you were holding a suitcase."

Toots blinked, her expression turning wistful—then sad, before shifting into a scowl. Finally, it settled into a wry smile. It was like watching all four weather seasons pass across her face.

"I was a wicked, wicked girl," she chortled.

Millie stared at her, wide-eyed.

Toots smiled wryly again. "You didn't know that about me? Yup, 'That girl's got a wild eye,' they used to say. After my mother divorced my father, she sent me off to one of those homes for 'wayward girls.'"

Toots snickered. "But there were a few 'wayward' men there, too."

Millie turned toward the window. As far as she was concerned, the conversation was over. It was no use. She could barely untangle her own emotions, let alone her mother's.

"Yep, a wicked, wicked girl," Toots said again.

Suddenly the car jolted, and Toots's arm shot out to block Millie from hitting the dash. A string of curse words followed, along with a repeated pumping of the brakes. The heavy traffic returned, and so did the tension in the car.

IT WAS AMAZING, really, how Ethel seemed to know the exact moment they'd arrive. GPS and cell phones hadn't even been invented, yet there she was on the front porch, peering down the street just as they rounded the corner. By the time they pulled into the driveway, she was already shuffling toward them, waving.

Millie was surprised by how short her aunt was—or had she shrunk over the years? She was barefoot, wearing a lavender paisley dress with a full-length, grandmotherly apron. A string of fake pearls hung around her neck, and every window of her trailer glowed with flickering electric candles as if it were Christmas in July.

Millie stepped out of the car.

"Goodness gracious," Ethel said. "Look at this girl, Harv'! She's sprouted up like a sunflower!"

Harvey appeared behind her in pleated trousers, a stained white T-shirt, and a formal hat—as if two different mothers had dressed him. He extended a hand to Millie then pulled her in for a gentle hug.

"Nice to see you, young lady. How was your trip? See anything interesting?"

Millie relaxed into his hug, remembering how safe she always felt with her uncle—like being with Leo.

"Nuh-uh, questions later," Ethel scolded, shaking a crooked finger at him. "Help these weary travelers with their bags! I'll show 'em to their room."

Millie stumbled up the porch steps but caught herself. Despite the warm welcome, the butterflies in her stomach were out of control.

"Well, here it is!" Ethel announced, swinging open a door to a room half-filled with boxes, a sewing machine, and bolts of fabric. The paneling was dark, and a faint smell of turpentine hung in the air. A few decorative touches tried to brighten the space: lace curtains in the window, crocheted doilies on every surface, and a splendid painting of Jesus on the wall. He stood on a stormy sea with arms spread wide toward a sinking fishing boat, where twelve terrified men clung to the sides.

"Sorry about the size of the room," Ethel said, glancing at Millie. "We're just a king and queen in a two-bedroom castle!"

Millie was never good at hiding her feelings. Her dread shone on her face like a neon sign. The twin bed was too small for her and her mother. They'd kill each other!

"Now don't get your hopes up, child," Ethel chuckled, her deep wrinkles folding around the whitest smile Millie had ever seen on an old lady. "This bed is for Toots. You and Pharaoh get the couch!"

Pharaoh—a skinny, perpetually shivering cat—sat nearby, clearly waiting for his chance to perch on a warm body.

While the adults retired to the kitchen to have tea and catch up, Millie prepared her sleeping spot. She covered the old tweed couch with linens, fluffed the pillows, and unpacked her nightie and toothbrush.

After finishing a glass of milk and a generous slice of Ethel's famous pudding cake, she changed and crawled under the sheets. Her belly was full... and even a little softer for Pharaoh.

In the kitchen, tension was heating up along with the tea water.

"The Good Book is clear about that!" Ethel shouted, loud enough to rattle the trailer's thin walls. "Everything hidden in darkness will come out in the light!"

*Bible quotes! Already!* They shot out of Ethel like rubber bullets —or pearls of wisdom, depending on one's perspective. In Toots's opinion, Ethel was an "ornery, self-righteous know-it-all." But to Millie, the woman was a superhero—the only relative who had the power of getting the last word with Toots.

It was a skill that Millie deeply admired.

The voices quieted, but the discussion stayed tense. *Politics!* Why was it such a hot-button issue for adults? Millie understood little about it and preferred it that way. To her, it always seemed like a silly back-and-forth game old people played, but no one ever truly won.

Toots launched into another rant about Nixon, and Millie groaned. Donkeys, elephants... it was so ridiculous. Neither held a candle to the *true* king of the jungle... *cats!*

"I vote for you, little guy," she whispered into Pharaoh's flicking ear. "A cat could rule the country, don't you think?"

Pharaoh purred in agreement, and Millie drifted off to sleep.

She woke to the soft scuffling of slippers. It was Ethel coming down the hall.

"Sorry, child," she whispered, seeing Millie's eyes open. "I just have to wee-wee."

Then it hit Millie—it was the middle of the night! Toots was asleep! She sat up fast, causing Pharaoh to leap off her belly. He landed on the carpet and glared with saucer eyes, clearly offended by the interruption to his beauty sleep. When Ethel came out of the bathroom, Millie was ready.

"Auntie," she said, peeking over the couch, "can we talk? I have something I need to ask you."

Ethel tilted her head, raising an eyebrow. "Oh? Well, another time, dear. It's late. Get some sleep."

Then she turned and shuffled back down the hall, like a caboose disappearing into a tunnel.

Millie flopped back with a groan. As far as she knew, that was the only train to truth she'd get... and it had just left the station without her.

# CHAPTER 8

# Solomon and the Half-Baby

The next morning, heavy drapes swooshed open, flooding the living room with eye-piercing sunlight.

"Uppy-uppy!" Ethel sang, clapping her hands. Millie groaned and pulled a pillow over her head.

"Oh no you don't," Ethel said, yanking it off. "My breakfasts don't wait."

Millie stretched, letting out an exaggerated yawn. When she finally shuffled into the kitchen, her hair was unbrushed and her mood was as rough as she looked.

"Look what the cat dragged in," Toots chortled. "It's about time."

Uncle Harvey pulled out the chair next to him. Millie sat down, staring blankly at a spread of scrambled eggs, biscuits, and a "bowl of ugly" she'd never encountered before: *grits.* Her stomach turned.

Toots, on the other hand, looked bright-eyed and well-rested. She leaned against the counter in a floral-print dress, with a large sunhat dangling down her back by a cord.

"So, Millie," Toots said, winking at Harvey over her teacup, "there's a steamboat ride this morning. Aunt Ethel doesn't feel up to it, so Harvey and I are going. You'll be fine here, won't you? They only have two tickets."

Millie shot her mother a disgusted glare. Was she *flirting* with Harvey?

Ethel, busy at the stove, turned around.

"Of course she'll be fine," she said, waving her hand like a queen summoning her court. "The girl still has sleepies in her eyes. You both go. We'll all go to the beach another day."

Millie flopped back onto the couch after breakfast, tugging at her sticky nightgown. What was her mother thinking, going to Florida in the summer? At least there were multiple fans stirring the thick air. Magazines on the nearby coffee table fluttered in the breeze, settling one way, then another.

Ethel fluttered as well, packing apples and tea cakes into a paper bag for Toots and Harvey.

"To tide you over 'til lunch," she said. She also made Harvey wear a hat, while teasing Toots about hers. "The whole boat's gonna get shade under that brim!"

Then, she practically shoved them out the door.

"Sit near the life preservers!" she shouted as she waved goodbye.

As soon as the door clicked shut, she spun around.

"Lord have mercy," she muttered, hurrying down the hallway. "I thought they'd never leave."

A moment later, she called out for Millie.

Following her aunt's voice, she found her in the master bedroom at the end of the hall. A rickety fan on a stand stirred the air, heavy with the scent of cigar-infused wool and cheap perfume. Ethel's back was turned as she rifled through a drawer full of loose papers, mumbling to herself.

"Ugh, I swear, paperwork is the devil's tool for frustrating an ol' woman!"

"I hate it too," Millie said, sitting on the edge of the bed. The dim room was lit only by the soft glow of a frilly lamp on the night-stand. Beneath it lay a Bible with an embroidered cover. Millie gently touched the lace edging, wishing she knew the Bible better. Her aunt made it sound interesting.

"Found it!" Ethel said, spinning around. She held up a thin magazine and chuckled. "I used to read this as a guilty pleasure back in Rochester."

Millie saw the title: *WE News—Rochester's Only News Magazine.*

Ethel paused, rubbing her lip thoughtfully. Then she dropped her hand and blurted out, "Do you feel like you don't belong, Millie? You know, to your family?"

Millie burst into tears. The question of all questions!

"Now, now, here," Ethel said, clucking as she handed her a handkerchief. "I could tell the minute I saw you, you were busting to talk. You're old enough to know the truth."

Millie wiped her eyes and sat up straighter. *Truth.* What a noble-sounding, terrifying word!

Ethel lowered herself onto a stool and flipped through the magazine until she landed on a dog-eared page.

"Here it is," she said, handing it over. "This article was published in October 1947, about ten months after you were born."

Millie read the headline:

*Children's Shelter Refuses to Discuss Report Woman Tries to Steal Illegitimate Baby.* \*

Ethel continued. "I couldn't believe it at first, but I knew it was you. It's your birthdate, your hospital; it explained all the rumors I'd been hearing."

Millie stared at the article, then at her aunt. Nothing was sinking in.

---

\*   For a copy of the entire article, see the website link given at the end of the book.

"*You're* the baby," Ethel said, tapping the magazine. "The one talked about right here."

She shifted uncomfortably on the stool and went on. "As I understand it, your birth mother wasn't much older than you are now when she got pregnant. Then she met Toots and moved in with her. Don't ask me how that happened; Toots wasn't speaking to me then. But later I heard a rumor that Toots promised to help her and pay her hospital bills. I'm sure Toots made her think she could keep you, too. But the two of them fought like badgers in a burrow. And well, now Toots has you. That's the short of it."

Millie stared wide-eyed at the headline. "She *stole* me?"

Ethel grimaced and hoisted herself up. "Move over, child. I may be seated in heavenly places, but this ol' bum needs a little cushioning."

Millie felt herself lift a few inches when Ethel settled beside her on the mattress.

"Yes," she said, "It does say that, and I believe there's some truth to it. But the article also says the stealing claim was dropped because an agreement was made. Although, I did some digging, and it wasn't legal what happened. You seemed to have slipped through the cracks, Millie—through the cracks of a shady deal that your birth mother was coerced into."

Ethel shifted again, her voice low and serious. "But it was the forties, you must understand; things like that happened a lot. And Toots... well, you know how she is. She can be mighty intimidating when she wants something."

Millie shook her head in disbelief and anger. Her entire life, being manipulated into believing a lie?

She ran her finger down the page, eyes narrowing. "It says here that she—my mother—lived with Toots. Do you know for how long?"

"About a year, from my figuring. Long enough to nurse you."

Millie's breath caught. "So... she left me?"

"Shut that mouth," Ethel snapped. But as soon as the words slipped out, regret flashed across her face. She softened her tone. "What I mean is, your mother didn't leave you, and you shouldn't think otherwise. This article proves that. Plus, no woman in her right mind can nurse a baby that long and not fall in love. Your mother was scared—threatened, even."

Ethel hung her head. "It must've been so hard."

Comforted for the moment, Millie skimmed the article. She noticed her birth mother had been kicked out at least once but came back. It *did* look like she was putting up a fight for her.

"Who wrote the letter to the magazine, Auntie? I don't see any names."

Ethel shrugged. "Don't know. Someone tried to intervene, though. I thought it was Mabel at first, but it wasn't. It must've been someone your birth mother knew—someone she confided in."

"And my mother's name—do you know it?"

Ethel tapped her temple, thinking. Then she grabbed the magazine.

"I do!" she said, flipping it over to the back. "I scribbled it down years ago while talking to Mabel. Here it is—*Jeanette Coyer*. I'm not sure about the spelling, but I heard she was a pretty girl, full of fun. By the way, Mabel knows about the article, and a little more than I do. We were waiting for the right time to tell you, sweetie. We knew Toots wouldn't 'fess up. She even threatened terrible things if we ever said anything."

"Oh, I promise I won't say anything to her about today," Millie blurted. "Not ever!"

Ethel shook her head. "Don't worry about me. I'm too old for anything to hurt me now. But you... you're still a minor. I don't want to see you kicked out on the street."

Millie nodded. Toots had already come close to doing that more than once.

"And my father?" she asked. "Do you know anything about him?"

"Not a thing." Ethel said with a shrug.

Just then, the phone rang. Ethel leapt up. "Uh-oh, that's probably Harv'! I told him to find a pay phone before they headed home."

"Thank you, Auntie," Millie said quickly, realizing her aunt had probably sacrificed her boat ticket so they could talk in private.

Ethel mumbled as she left the room, "Solomon and the half-baby... by golly, Solomon and the half-baby..."

Millie stayed behind, studying the article. So many nameless strangers fighting over what to do with her life? It was so strange! And while Ethel's reference to "Solomon and the half-baby" was lost on her—a Bible story she wasn't familiar with yet—Millie instinctively knew she *had* to have been affected by such a tumultuous entrance into the world. How could a baby *not* feel the tension of two women fighting for the final word in her life? Or not feel guilty enjoying one mother's arms while the other looked on with jealousy? Could a baby ever feel whole, when who she truly belonged to was always in question?

A ball of confused feelings lay heavy in Millie's stomach. From the kitchen came the sounds of clanking pots, followed by Ethel's voice, "Don't dillydally in there—they'll be home soon!"

A moment later: "I mean it, right now! And put that magazine away. I don't even want to think about what Toots would do if she found out you saw it!"

Millie rose, and with trembling hands returned the magazine to the drawer. Her aunt was right. That was one thing she didn't want to think about either.

# CHAPTER 9

## Last Words

L unch felt like a blur. Millie was silent, lost in thought. Toots, on the other hand, was buzzing with energy from her time with Harvey and already eager for the next adventure.

"Millie-Millie-Millie," she said, poking her daughter with a bread stick. "What do you want to do this afternoon? How about Busch Gardens? They have *flowers*. You *love* flowers!"

Millie offered a flat "whatever" without looking up from her plate. It didn't matter what she wanted. She didn't "love" flowers—*Toots* did. She wasn't in control—*Toots* was.

So, they went to Busch Gardens.

But Millie was determined to get through it—to get through the entire vacation—without revealing the fodder in her brain. She kept her face blank (or so she thought), and her words icy. She wasn't ready to start a fire with Toots that might turn into an inferno.

Fortunately, she'd have a chance to let off some steam at her happy place before the vacation ended.

"Over there," Toots said, pointing with her umbrella to a spot in the sand. Millie, head down, weaved through the crowded beach until Toots pointed again. "Right there, hurry up! My feet are burning! I hope this circus woman gets out of our way!"

Millie cringed. The woman wasn't much bigger than Toots—and within earshot. Just then, a child darted in front of them chasing a beach ball.

Toots stopped to scold him. "Little boy, watch where you're going!"

When Millie reached the spot and dropped their gear, she couldn't hold back. "*Really*, Mother? Did you have to make a scene?"

But Toots wasn't behind her. She had fallen behind to pick up another little boy, still in diapers, who had stumbled in front of her.

"Whoops-a-daisy," she said, brushing him off. Then she turned to a nearby girl and complimented her bathing suit.

Millie spread her blanket and shook her head. Toots was such a conundrum. How could someone be rude one moment and charming the next?

She dug her feet into the sand and closed her eyes... her breathing slowing. The symphony of children's laughter, waves lapping, and seagulls squawking slowly did its calming magic. Toots plopped down beside her, crossing her legs on her blanket. She sifted through her purse, muttering about her rings. When she finally found them, she turned onto her belly with a groan. Millie could feel her eyes drilling into her.

"Cripes, Millie, put your sunhat on. It's a hundred degrees out!"

Millie wasn't about to be an obedient daughter. She grabbed her shell bag and stood up.

"I'm going for a walk," she said.

Toots glanced at her watch, then pointed toward the bathhouse. "Go that way. Look for Harvey and Ethel; they'll be here soon."

Millie wandered along the shore, kicking at the cool water. She paused to let the tide tug at her feet, cementing them into the sand.

A small shell caught her eye. She bent down to pick it up, admiring its iridescent sheen and spiral interior. But its edges were chipped, so she tossed it back into the sea and watched it sink.

A wave of sadness swept over her. Was she a little shell... broken, imperfect, discarded into the vast ocean of life by forces bigger than herself? She didn't want to be worthless or rejected. She didn't want to drown in even more unanswered questions.

She wiped away a tear and kept walking. A familiar voice called out.

"Yoo-hoo, Millie! Over here!"

It was Ethel, with Harvey close behind. Even without hearing them, Millie would've spotted them. Both were wearing matching straw hats, oversized sunglasses, and Hawaiian shirts so garish they looked out of place—even in Florida. Though they'd left New York state years ago, they still acted like Yankee tourists.

"I declare," Ethel panted, dropping her bag. "I wasn't sure how we'd find you in this crowd!"

Millie picked up her bag and offered her arm.

"Oh, thank you, dear," Ethel said, hooking onto her. "I can see why Jesus said that sand is a poor foundation for a house. I can't even walk on it! So, how are you doing? Holding up?"

Millie shrugged, flashing a fake smile. They were already at Toots's spot.

Harvey, eager to cool off, hurried straight for the water.

"You forgot your floatie!" Ethel called after him, but his bony legs were already knee-deep in the surf.

"He's such a terrible swimmer," Ethel said as she unfolded her chair. She glanced at Toots, who was watching Harvey. "Go babysit him, would you Toots? I'm afraid he needs a stronger woman than Millie to keep him from drowning!"

Worded that way, Toots couldn't resist. She laughed and sprang to her feet.

"I'm coming!" she shouted to Harvey, who was now splashing around doing a pitiful impression of drowning.

Ethel clapped her hands, rocking with laughter. "That man, I tell you, he's gonna be baptized for good one of these days!"

"Auntie," Millie said softly, her heart picking up pace. She knew moments alone with her aunt were rare, and one question weighed heavily on her. "Why couldn't my mother just keep me?"

"Tsk, tsk, child," Ethel said. She adjusted her chair, scooting closer while keeping an eye on Toots and Harvey. "Listen up, I've told you before. Your mother was just a scared young thing when she had you; probably couldn't tell her parents, either. It was a big disgrace to be pregnant out of wedlock in the forties. Most girls hid their bump as long as they could, then skipped town to go to one of those... 'homes for unwed mothers.'"

Ethel paused, her voice trembling. "You must understand something, Millie. There wasn't much support for a woman in her situation. It was hard... real hard. At the home, you didn't even get a chance to say a proper goodbye before..."

She stopped, dabbing at a tear that slipped between the creases of her face.

"All you can do is pray for the little guy," she continued, her gaze drifting wistfully across the horizon. "You pray for him. Every single day. For the rest of your life."

Millie stared at her aunt, a woman of eighty-five years, with a roadmap of joys and losses etched into her face. Whatever memory she was recalling, it was clearly sacred. Millie didn't know what to say.

Ethel laughed suddenly, her composure returning as she spotted Harvey and Toots emerging from the water. "Hallelujah, you both survived!"

Before they returned to their towels, she leaned over and said one last thing. "Keep this in mind, Millie: if you want to find your birth mother, you should try. Don't be afraid. It might be hard, but the truth will set you free."

*The truth will set you free.*

The phrase lingered in the salty air, its energy pulsing in Millie's ears.

Unfortunately, there were no more chances to talk to Ethel during the Florida trip. Millie's remaining questions would have to wait... hopefully for a long-distance phone call from a payphone in New York.

It was a call that never happened. Shortly after they returned home, Ethel suffered a stroke that stole her ability to speak. Less than a year later, Harvey called with the news: Ethel had peacefully passed through the pearly gates she had spoken of so often, to meet the God she had so fervently believed in.

Millie would never forget her aunt's boldness—and how she sacrificed her boat ticket to give her the truth.

# CHAPTER 10

# A City in Turmoil

It was just a joke to her friends—something four teenagers could goof around with on a drizzly July day.

For Millie, however, when the strange little board was placed on the floor, she saw its potential right away. Two years had passed since the Florida trip, and a cloud of unanswered questions still hung over her seventeen-year-old head. Would a witch board talk to her? It seemed worth a try.

The girls sat in a tight circle, with the shades drawn for a spooky effect. After a few minutes of fooling around, Nellie leaned forward.

"What does it say?" she asked, smirking as she tugged the planchette toward her. "I know! It spells, 'Over my dead body!'"

The other girls giggled.

"Stop it," Millie snapped, slapping at Nellie's hand. Nellie gave a quick, nervous laugh as she stood up to leave.

A redhead named Sue piped up. "Ouija boards are stupid. It isn't making any sense. Come on, girls, let's go shopping!"

Sue, the oldest of the group, was the pitcher for the girls' community softball team Millie had joined. Thin as a stick and pale as a ghost, Sue had an attitude to match her fiery red hair. One time, she and Millie had gotten into a petty argument. Words turned to slaps, slaps turned to pushes, and the two girls rolled in the dirt until Millie pinned Sue down. Later, they laughed about it... how "Pencil Sue" was no match for "Mighty Millie!"

In persuasion, though, Sue was top dog. The girls always leaned toward her opinions over Millie's. The moment Sue mentioned shopping, they scrambled to find their purses, powder their noses, and put on their shoes.

Another teammate, Jessica Swanson, wasn't moving as fast.

"Do you really think it's safe to drive out there?" she asked, wringing her hands. "Chad got beat up on Saturday, you know. He had to get twenty stitches in his face."

Jessica, or "Batty," as she was called on the field, was practically a midget—and short on courage, too. But as an outfielder, she was outstanding. Whenever a ball flew her way, she darted like a hungry bat and snatched it from the air.

Sue rolled her eyes. "Gee whiz, Jess, how long are you gonna be afraid of everything except a softball? Plus, we all know your brother's a hothead. He probably had it coming."

The truth was, Jessica wasn't the only one on edge; all the girls were. Just days earlier, Rochester had erupted in an unprecedented wave of racial violence that began Friday, July 24th, 1964. Most of the city's frightened residents sought refuge in their homes, glued to radios and TVs, watching mobs of enraged rioters march through and ransack large areas of the Third and Seventh wards. Five people had died, and several hundred had been injured.

Jessica ignored Sue's jab at her brother and asked the question again, this time directing to the next girl in the pecking order. "So, what do you think, Millie? Is it safe out there?"

Millie puffed her chest out. "It's fine. Midtown is open for business, and we'll all stick together."

Then she walked outside to find Nellie, who was smoking while leaning against Sue's car.

"A humble gift," Sue called her yellow beauty, a 1964 Ford Mustang her parents had given her on graduation day. To the other girls, it sounded like a boast. None of them would've imagined getting a car for graduation, let alone a "humble" Mustang. And especially not Millie—she hadn't even graduated. By ninth grade she'd played hooky so often that she figured she might as well make a career of it!

"You're going to keep your mouth shut, right?" Millie asked Nellie, pulling a pack of cigarettes and a lighter from her purse. She opened the car door and motioned for Nellie to get in. She could hear the other girls coming. *"You do know* Sue's dad is on the police force, don't you? They're still prosecuting people from the riot."

Nellie climbed into the rear seat and slid over to the other side. "I know, I know. You don't have to keep reminding me. I won't say anything. But come on, wouldn't it be so fun to tell the girls?"

Millie's frown cracked. Telling the girls that she and Nellie had instigated the infamous race riot in Rochester? That would be fun, even if it *was* a ludicrous boast.

Although, the truth was just as outrageous.

On the infamous Friday night, Nellie's oldest sister, who was dating a Black man, was throwing a party in his front yard. Nothing had seemed out of the ordinary at first, except for the oppressive heat, stifling humidity, and a full moon. Nellie and Millie had been innocently sipping homemade hooch and dancing with some beat-niks when suddenly there was an angry mob moving down Joseph Avenue! Moments later the two of them were handcuffed and tossed into the back of a paddy wagon, wailing out their story of innocence to an overwhelmed police officer. Fortunately, their tears worked. They had been released without being arrested and spent the rest of the weekend in their homes, telling no one what had happened.

"Just let things die down first," Millie said, sliding in next to Nellie. Sue and Jessica stood outside, smoking.

"Damn, this car's cramped," Millie said. "Sue's parents are airheads; a sports car is so impractical."

"Geez, what's eating you?" Nellie asked. "You've been kinda mean lately. Is it about your search? Did you find something out?"

Millie took a long drag on her cigarette then flicked it out the window. Nellie could be annoying at times, but aside from Patrick, she was the only friend Millie could trust with details. She already heard about the second call Millie made to Patrick's mother, Aunt Mabel—a call that was *not* muffled with static like the first one—and how her aunt had *finally* shared what little she knew about Millie's birth. This included confirming her birth mother's name, her age, and her city of birth.

It was enough information to find her... or so Millie thought.

"No, nothing new," she replied. "I've checked everywhere I can think of. Plus, Aunt Mabel isn't sure she has the spelling of her name right. I'm sure *that* doesn't help."

"Did you find the homeless shelter mentioned in the article? Did you try the hospital?"

Millie shook her head. "Dead ends. They either don't know or have impossible hoops for me to jump through."

"Phone books?"

Millie sighed. Nellie always had the same questions.

"Of course," she replied impatiently. "I checked both Syracuse *and* Rochester. And no, nobody knows anything about my father, either."

As Sue and Jessica approached the car, Millie hurried to end the conversation.

"But I've already accepted all that, Nellie. I'm not looking anymore, so don't worry about me. I'm just in a mood."

Once everyone piled into the car, Jessica fiddled with the radio dial.

"Stop—go back!" Sue squealed, swatting Jessica's hand away. She turned the dial back to the throaty, soulful voice of Aretha Franklin. "I love the Queen!"

Groans from the others quickly gave way to wide eyes and rocking torsos. They belted out the lyrics in unison:

*"Groovin' down a crowded avenue, doin' anything we like to do. There's always lots of things that we can see; we can be anyone we like to be."*

The song couldn't have been more perfect!

"Where are we going?" Jessica asked as Sue passed the turnoff to Midtown.

Sue was silent, gripping the steering wheel. She cast a glance at Millie through the rearview mirror.

"Roll up your windows and lock the doors," Millie said sternly to the girls. Jessica slouched and whimpered. Millie, on the other hand, sat up straighter with gleaming eyes. Sue was heading straight into the war zone!

"Stop it, Jess," Sue said. "And sit up. You're making me look like a chauffeur. I just want to see how bad it is."

Once in the area, Sue turned off the radio and crept the car like she was on a safari. They passed buildings with shattered windows, torn-down signs, and parking lots strewn with debris. In the distance, a thin column of smoke rising from a smoldering fire curled up into the gray sky.

"How awful," Nellie whispered. "It looks like the apocalypse."

Millie tapped Sue on the shoulder. "This is as far as we should go."

Up ahead, the street was clogged with police cars and uniformed men who were stringing yellow tape across driveways and around buildings.

Annoyed, Sue veered sharply onto the next side street and rolled her eyes—a gesture Millie didn't catch.

"So, where are we going first?" Nellie asked when they finally pulled into the plaza.

Sue found a place to park and everyone sighed in relief. The parking lot, stretched out before the towering retail stores, was eerily quiet and clean. Sue pointed to a brick structure ahead and replied, "B. Foreman's, of course!"

Millie opened her mouth to suggest McCurdy's instead, but not because she thought it a better store. The only reason she could have justified the suggestion was because Leo worked there as a night watchman—had been for many years. No, Millie just didn't want to defer to Sue like the others.

Before her argument came out, however, everyone was reaching for their door handles.

Millie exited the car and walked toward the entrance faster than the others.

"First one there's a rotten egg!" she shouted back.

Laughter erupted behind her, followed by Nellie's voice, "You mean the last one, Millie, the *last* one there's a rotten egg!"

Inside the revolving doors, cool, sterile air greeted the girls, infused with the alluring scent of new clothes, perfume, and something Millie had a particularly keen nose for: *clearance sales.*

She grabbed Nellie by the elbow.

"Follow me," she whispered, steering her toward the back of the store where she knew the sale racks were. "Let's lose those clowns."

But within minutes, Sue reappeared with Jessica trailing behind, lecturing everyone on how they should dress for their body types. Millie rolled her eyes and wandered off alone. It was the only way she knew to avoid literally dressing Sue with a black eye.

Back in the car at their agreed-upon time, the girls eagerly showed off their treasures.

*"The color of this poncho is divine!"*

*"I can't believe I snagged these pumps for five dollars."*

*"Aren't these earrings groovy?"*

Jessica noticed Millie's unusual silence.

"You didn't buy anything, Mil'?" she asked.

Millie held up her empty hands. "You know me—broke as a church mouse."

Nellie clapped her hands together, knowing Millie better than anyone. "You stole something, didn't you!?"

Sue and Jessica joined in, clapping and chanting, "Show us! Show us!"

Millie caved.

"Okay, okay," she said sheepishly. She bent down and rolled up a pant leg—then another and another. *Three layers of slacks!*

The girls roared with laughter and Nellie snorted. Millie turned her head to the window. Behind her sunglasses, a single tear slipped out.

Stealing wasn't something she liked to do, especially not once the guilt kicked in. She didn't even need to steal. Toots occasionally gave her money for what she needed. Rather, it was an urge she couldn't control, which when she gave into, made her feel oddly in control.

The contradiction scared her.

"I have a groovy idea," Sue said, grinning wryly at Millie in the rearview mirror. "You should wear all those layers to make your beau work for it!"

There it was again, another dig. Unlike the other girls, Millie didn't have a boyfriend. *And Sue knew it.*

As soon as the car stopped at an intersection, Millie leaped out and slammed the door behind her. Anger coursed through her, making the two-mile walk home pass quickly. She hadn't even noticed that the store tag on her inner slacks rubbed her skin raw.

Millie headed straight to the kitchen with one goal: numb herself with macaroni and cheese. Carrying the steaming pot into the living room, she settled on the couch, placing a thick towel on her lap first. Toots was nearby rocking in front of the TV, her hands wrapping, looping, and transforming a skein of yarn into a long row of crocheted roses.

Millie dove in, taking her first spoonful. Mayor Lamb's face appeared on the screen with a scrolling ticker beneath him that read: "*National Guard deployed. Massive city clean-up begins.*"

"What do you have there?" Toots asked sharply.

Millie froze mid-chew. Something felt off. Toots was rocking aggressively, her eyes locked onto her clashing crochet needles. Even Ladybug, after twelve years of living close to the floor, knew what certain vibrations meant. He was already in his safe spot: a well-worn pillow under the end table.

"Mac and cheese," Millie said, quickly swallowing. She stood, wrapped the towel around the pot, and headed for the attic.

"It looks big enough to drown a horse," Toots snickered. Then she added, "Is it big enough to drown Leo? That no-good excuse of a man is as useless as a..."

*Ugh.* Millie hadn't even reached the stairs when one of Toots's dirtiest similes rang out, clearly loud enough for Leo to hear. He was in the other room, trying to sleep before his night shift.

When Millie reached the attic, she stripped off her clothes—stolen and otherwise—and tossed everything into the closet. Then she sat on the bed in her underwear and resumed her meal, silently scolding herself that a fat girl should make better food choices.

A wacky thought then popped into her head.

*Being in a giant pot drowning in cheese wouldn't be such a bad way to go!*

# CHAPTER 11

## Freddy Flad

Millie hung up the phone, moving sluggishly. It was Friday night and she had just turned down an invitation to go roller skating with Nellie and her steady.

"It's your date night," Millie had told Nellie. "I'd just be a third wheel."

A lame excuse, really. Chuck was a teddy bear—the friendliest man she'd ever met. If she hadn't felt so gloomy and grungy, she probably would've enjoyed herself.

Instead, she poured a glass of orange juice, grabbed a plate of pumpkin muffins, and headed toward the attic stairs. Toots, passing by with a laundry basket, stopped her.

"Someone is coming over this afternoon. I want you to meet him."

"Uh-huh, sure," Millie mumbled, not looking up.

"Be ready by four," she called after her. "And don't be dressed in those old rags!"

*That's odd,* Millie thought. *Toots has never wanted to introduce me to one of her male visitors before.*

In the attic, Millie decided to take a late-morning nap. She put a stack of records on the turntable, leaving a trail of muffin crumbs as she crawled into bed. Depression was creeping in—she knew it instinctively—and her life was being squandered. She was practically an adult at seventeen, and all she did was lie around daydreaming while playing the same sad story in her head repeatedly. It all kept her too busy to care. It was like the Beatles sang on one of her records:

*There's a place*
*Where I can go*
*When I feel low,*
*When I feel blue.*
*And it's my mind,*
*And there's no time,*
*When I'm alone.*

But what *had* become dangerous—and slowly eroding Millie's sanity—was how her daydreaming had morphed into *darkdreaming*. And it was happening yet again as she drifted in and out of sleep, the dimming afternoon sun casting a shadowy figure at the foot of her bed... and in her imagination.

She should've ignored it—found something healthier to focus on—but as usual, she indulged it. The idea that these "beings," as she perceived them, were nefarious, never crossed her mind. But later in life Millie would see them as evil spirits who wanted to destroy her. They promised comfort and a distraction from her pain but always left her with emptiness and self-loathing.

A shout from downstairs interrupted her. "You'd better be dressed up there, Millie! He'll be here soon!"

Millie pulled a blanket over her head.

*I should probably get up*, she thought. *She might be planning on leaving Leo for this guy!*

With a heavy sigh, she got out of bed and pulled on capris and a T-shirt. She waited for the doorbell to ring, then slowly made her way down the stairs.

She hadn't expected to see the person standing there.

"Hey," he said with a small wave.

When Millie locked eyes with the visitor, he smiled shyly—or was it slyly? It was hard to tell. She recognized him from the butcher shop a few blocks away—Freddy Flad. Hard to forget a name like that. She'd always assumed he was older than her, and way out of her league. Not that she believed any guy was in her league.

Toots clapped her hands together.

"I thought you two kids would like to hang out," she said, winking at Freddy. Then she turned to Millie. "He likes music, honey. Why don't you show him your records?"

Freddy smiled again. He was ridiculously cute. He wore bell-bottom jeans, a yellow cardigan over a tight white T-shirt, and he had a distinctly Italian face that blushed like a ripe tomato.

Millie asked him what kind of music he liked, and then—partly to ease the awkwardness in the room and partly to escape the stupid look on Toots's face—she agreed to bring him upstairs.

It was a mistake.

Before long, the handsome visitor lost interest in her music collection, grew tired of small talk, and made it clear he hoped for something else from his visit.

That night Millie cried herself to sleep. Sure, she had known what sex was from an early age. Among many of her relatives—especially with Toots—sex was discussed openly and without any modesty. It was more like lingerie flapping from a flagpole: shameless, bawdy, and always turning something innocent into something shocking or crude.

But even with all that exposure—and worse, the abuse she'd experienced as a child—Millie wasn't prepared for what real sex really meant. The emotional weight alone was more than she'd imagined. When Freddy slipped downstairs and out the door, a sharp pang stabbed her heart. She knew she'd never see him again.

Then there was the other cost to be paid... the *big* one.

A few weeks later, it would nearly choke the life out of her in a convenience store bathroom stall.

*Oh God, it can't be!* Millie cried. She gripped the test strip with one hand and clutched her chest with the other. *I'm pregnant!*

She rocked on the toilet seat, moaning. It felt like a boa constrictor was squeezing her chest. Her thoughts spiraled.

*What should I do? Run away? Where? With what money? Should I end it all? Tempting, but...*

A knock on the door startled her.

"You a'ight in there, baby? Need me to call somebody fo' you?"

It was Janice, the store owner—a big, Black, shamelessly pushy woman who clearly knew what was going on. Millie had bought the test from her, after all.

"I'm fine," Millie sniffled. "I'll be out in a minute."

Her mind raced. She had to tell someone, but who? Patrick? He cared for her, but he was wrapped up with a new boyfriend. Nellie and Chuck were out of town at a Rolling Stones concert. No, she needed someone who could help right away. *Someone who would understand.*

Then she remembered Sue, from the softball team.

After Toots went to bed that evening, Millie slipped out, crossed the street, and ducked into the phone booth. She shivered in the cool spring air as she dialed Sue's number.

"Hello?" Sue answered groggily.

Millie poured out her distressing news. "I'm really scared, Sue. What should I do?"

The following pause made her stomach tighten. They hadn't talked in a while; Millie had snubbed both her and Jessica after their last outing. Soon after that, Sue got pregnant out of wedlock and her so-called "good" Catholic parents sent her away. When she came back, she claimed to have miscarried... although rumors swirled about an abortion. Millie didn't know what to believe, except that Sue had returned different. Broken-in-the-head different. She had become withdrawn, moody, and often wore some of her clothes inside out.

Sue finally spoke. "There's only one thing to do, Millie. You have to tell your mother. You may not think so now, but you need support. My mom was mad at first, but she came around. Honestly, I think I was born a love child."

Sue chuckled awkwardly, and Millie almost argued: *Support? You don't know my mother!*

Sue did have her own baggage, though. Her mother was a lush and her father a workaholic. Sue had practically raised herself.

"I guess you're right," Millie muttered, wiping her sleeve across her eyes. Toots would likely hunt her down if she tried to skip town.

As her dime neared its end, Millie asked Sue where she went and what happened to her baby. Sue went cold, dodging the questions with a dismissive script: "Life is shitty sometimes, you know? I was given my options, and it is what it is."

Millie hung up and stepped out of the phone booth. She was still shivering, but at least she wasn't hyperventilating.

*Options,* she whispered, hurrying back to the house and crawling into bed. *I can deal with options.*

"WHERE'S FREDDY?" Millie demanded.

She stood in the kitchen wearing pajamas, feet planted in a fighter's stance. Her hair was a snake's nest, and her mood just as venomous. She'd just woken from a vivid nightmare where her mother's hand controlled Freddy like a puppet, making him tell jokes to a roaring, stark-naked audience. It had felt so real that Millie half expected to see him sitting on Toots's lap that morning!

"What?" Toots snapped, bending to open a cupboard. "Why should I care?"

"Because I'm pregnant," Millie blurted. "I already took a test and it's his—Freddy's."

Leo was sitting at the table sipping coffee. He blinked rapidly, but despite the shock, he stared blankly over his cup.

Toots dropped a lid, the clatter sending Ladybug fleeing. She left it on the floor and paced back and forth while repeatedly muttering, "Okay, okay…"

Millie pulled out a chair and slumped into it like a rag doll, all the fight gone out of her.

Toots stopped at the junk drawer for a pen.

"Okay," she repeated, scribbling on a notepad. "Looks like it'll be around March. I'll make an appointment with the doctor right away."

"And you," she said, pointing at Leo. "You need to ask that idiot boss of yours for a raise! Babies cost money, and money doesn't grow on trees."

Leo remained silent.

"So that's it?" Millie said, "You're not sending me away? Not putting the baby up for adoption? What about Freddy? Shouldn't he know?"

Toots put her hands on her hips. "Freddy's a jerk. We don't need him. Besides, he and his swindling father are moving the business back to Jersey. They're as good as dead to me."

Millie left the kitchen, feeling a migraine coming on. She stretched out on the couch and picked up a *Better Homes and Gardens* magazine from the coffee table. As she flipped through the pages, her thoughts ran wild.

*At least Toots didn't blow her top,* she thought. *But how am I going to raise a baby, in this house, with Toots? I'm only seventeen. I have no job. I have no husband...*

Abruptly, her internal monologue stopped. Right in front of her, in the magazine, was a beautiful photograph of a mother, daughter, and granddaughter—three generations of female ranchers—gathered around a red filly mare in a historic barn stall.

How vivid it felt! She could almost smell the horse's hair, the fresh hay, and the musky leather saddle. The little girl on the horse looked about the same age Millie had been when she took riding lessons. Why hadn't she continued? It seemed like a lifetime ago now.

She went on to read the article, but then it weighed heavy on her all day. It wasn't the story that was troubling her; it was something else... something harder to pinpoint.

When it finally hit her, it was in the middle of a sleepless night.

"Oh my God," she whispered, bolting upright in bed. Goosebumps rose on her arms. "Could it be that Toots *wanted* me to get pregnant? Is that why she invited Freddy to the house?"

Another gasp. "Oh no, maybe it's worse than that! Maybe she wanted me to have a baby so *she* could have the baby!"

Millie fell back on her pillow, draping her arm across her eyes. *Raise a child with Toots? Like Jeanette tried to do when she lived with her?*

No. No. No. It was such a horrid thought—all of it. She tried to push it away, but it was too late.

The suspicion had taken root... and it would grow.

# CHAPTER 12

# *Fanny Farmer*

"Hello, my name is Stella," said a woman with smiling eyes. She held out a tray of chocolates and bowed low to match Millie's height. "Go ahead. You can have one of each if you'd like."

Stella was the public relations director at the Fanny Farmer candy factory when Millie toured it for a fourth-grade field trip. When Stella invited Millie to sample from the tray—an offer Millie believed was just for her—she liked her instantly. Stella's voice was kind, her perfume exquisite, and she carried her plump, mature body as if royalty ran in her blood.

Millie thought of that day, and of Stella, when she told her mother she wanted a job. Toots had no argument; her agreeableness likely due to the fact Millie had become moody, combative, and impossible to live with since finding out she was pregnant.

Plus, they both knew Leo was *never* going to get that raise.

"You can take a seat over there," a receptionist said when Millie, now eighteen, walked into the factory. She pointed to a waiting area. "The assistant manager is still in a meeting but should be done shortly."

Millie sat down, surrounded by the soft buzz of elevator music. Huge, colorful posters hung on the walls, featuring mouth-watering collages of fudges, mints, fruit jellies, and just about every temptation that could be covered or filled with chocolate.

*What was I thinking, applying for a job at a candy factory?* Millie thought, shifting uncomfortably in her chair. Her legs itched and prickled against the rough tweed fabric. *And what possessed me to wear shorts?*

She glanced at her belly, dreading the day she could no longer hide it.

"Mildred Saxe?" a voice called.

Millie stood and walked toward the woman in the doorway. As she shook hands, her mouth dropped open. It was Stella! She still worked there—older and grayer, of course—and just as beautiful as Millie remembered.

"Okay, Mildred, let's learn a little about you," Stella said as she lowered herself behind a large desk simply topped with a clipboard, a pencil cup, and a small cactus blooming with a white flower.

"Everybody calls me Millie," Millie said. She wanted that clear from the start. She considered asking if Stella remembered her but thought better of it.

"Thank you for telling me," Stella said warmly. After a few questions, she leaned back and nodded. "Okay, Millie, I think we can make something work. If you don't mind starting on the tail end, I could use help on the east-wing packaging line. By 'tail,' I mean it's at the bottom of everyone's picklist. Kiddy Pops, you know, nothing exciting—but there's been a swell of orders lately. Would that suit you for now? I'd love to start you tomorrow."

Stella flashed a smile, sliding a paper and pen across the desk.

Millie was taken aback by Stella's smile. She had crooked teeth but didn't seem to mind! Millie had a similar imperfection: a "middle-child" incisor that, over time, had been pushed out by its siblings. She'd always been self-conscious about the way it protruded, but when Stella smiled, Millie found herself smiling back... wider than she had in a long time.

"Sure. I can start tomorrow," Millie said.

After a few days, though, she understood Stella's warning. Wrapping lollipops *was* boring. Grab, wrap, twist, and drop—over and over as fast as you could. Worse yet, she was seated with a cliquish brood of young hens who decided to treat the new girl like she had a disease.

*I'm an adult, I'm making money*, she reminded herself every time she pulled on her smock and hairnet. *Let the hens cluck. I will wrap on!*

That is, until the line clogged!

The girls had always made it sound like a dreaded occurrence, but Millie never imagined it would happen to her—and especially not in her first week. When she heard the crunching noise and saw the conveyor belt stop, her heart also stopped.

Stella and a floor manager arrived on the scene together.

"I keep telling Millie she needs to twist around the stick more, but she won't listen," one of the girls complained, ensuring Stella could hear.

Millie shot her a glare. This girl had been bossy from day one, a ringleader of sorts who spent every break in the smoking room flirting and talking dirty. Millie avoided the room. She had quit smoking when she got pregnant and even the smell made her sick.

The manager ignored the accusation.

"Fifteen minutes!" he barked, sending the girls scampering. Millie headed for the exit, hoping to find a bench outside to sit alone.

Stella stopped her. "Join me in my office, Millie. I'd like to talk to you."

Millie sat stiffly in the chair and opened her mouth to defend herself, but Stella spoke first.

"I just want you to know, Millie, you're doing a good job. Don't let the other girls worry you. That machine has been acting up lately, even before you came."

Millie closed her mouth, relieved.

"Are you okay with the line?" Stella asked. "Because if not, I can switch things around."

Millie assured her she was fine. She didn't want Stella to think she was a quitter!

Stella smiled and leaned back in her chair. "That's a pretty necklace you're wearing."

Millie gently touched the cross around her neck. It had been a gift from Aunt Mabel—one she especially liked because it had a tiny red rose in the center.

"Thank you," Millie said, then returned the compliment about Stella's scarf. It was one she had admired before, with a particular shade of blue that made Stella's eyes shimmer like pools.

Stella laughed, pulling the wrap tighter around her neck. "Oh, thank you, dear. It is a pretty color, isn't it? I also like that it hides my double chin."

"I wish I could hide a few things too," Millie said sheepishly, glancing down at her curves. It was hard to imagine anyone *not* thinking she was pregnant.

"A-lines and tucks, my dear," Stella said, standing up to show her figure from the side. "I've got some weight too, but you need to work with it, not against it. See how the tailoring on this blouse creates the illusion of a waist? It's often better to accentuate your shape than to hide it."

She sat back down. "I *hope* you know you're a pretty girl, Millie. I *hope* you always remember that."

*Hope...* what a lovely word. Unlike some other four-letter words

Millie heard at home and work, *hope* felt like a gentle breeze. Just hearing it made her feel lighter, less worried... *less pregnant.*

"I'll try," Millie said, relaxing into her chair. She hoped the break wasn't over yet.

Stella looked at her watch but didn't seem affected by it. She asked Millie if she had pets, then shared that she had four cats but refused to collect any more. She admitted to collecting brooches, however, which she pinned all over her bedroom curtains. Summoning her courage, Millie asked about Stella's perfume and learned it was called White Diamonds. She also learned that Stella indulged in reading fashion magazines in the bathtub, dreaming about starting a clothing line for bigger women.

Millie soaked up Stella's words like a sponge. When she finally returned to her station, the line was already running. She'd been in Stella's office for over twenty minutes! She couldn't remember ever having a conversation so grown-up, so full of positivity. It made her want to be a better person.

In fact, after Millie finished her shift that day, she stopped by the library to borrow books on how to dress better. The changes she made were small at first: tying a belt around her waist, wearing a skirt instead of shorts; but each day she persevered and made bolder choices. Even Toots took an interest, pulling out her sewing machine and tailoring some of Millie's clothes.

Stella would sometimes notice these changes and compliment Millie. Then one day, in the hearing of the other girls, Stella declared her to be one of the best-dressed employees Fanny Farmer ever had! Millie beamed. It brought back the feeling of being seven again, hurrying downstairs every Saturday afternoon wearing her white rider chaps and silver-buckled leather vest to turn on the Sally Star show. She never wanted to miss her heroine's famous sign-on: *"I hope you feel as good as you look—'cause you sure look good to your gal, Sal!"*

Sadly, Millie's "fashion-venturous" days at the factory were short-lived. After just a few months on the job, she could no longer ignore what was happening. Her bouts of morning sickness were turning into all-day, every-day sickness. Something wasn't right.

*She had to tell her mother.*

# CHAPTER 13

# Double-Take

D r. Sloan, the family physician, slowly lowered his clipboard. He had just finished jotting down his examination results when he peered solemnly over the top of his glasses.

"I'm sorry to be the bearer of bad news, Millie," he said, his bushy brows knit with concern. "But I believe you have toxemia."

Toots, who was sitting nearby with her head in her hands, unleashed a stream of curse words.

The doctor raised a hand to quiet her. This wasn't his first dealing with Toots.

"Mrs. Saxe, please calm down. I'm referring Millie to a prenatal specialist right away. He'll determine the best course of action to reduce the risk to both her and the baby."

Millie's head throbbed so badly, even her thoughts hurt. *Her life was at risk? The baby's, too? And what the hell was toxemia?*

The rest of the afternoon passed in a blur. Toots drove her straight to the hospital for tests, where the diagnosis was confirmed. Yes, Millie had toxemia, a potentially serious complication affecting a small percentage of pregnancies.

She also learned something else. The ultrasound revealed not just one baby—but *two* babies inside her!

The moment the ultrasound nurse left, the prenatal doctor walked in. Millie blurted out, "Are they going to die?"

Getting to the point only seemed logical; the day was dragging on and Toots had shut down. She just stood in the corner, her face ashen and distant.

The doctor gave Millie a reassuring pat. "We're going to think positive, young lady. But it will be tricky. The goal is to keep you pregnant as long as possible. But if your symptoms worsen, we may have to induce labor early."

He lowered the railing of the bed so she could step out. "For now, stay home and get plenty of bed rest. And I know nausea is a big issue but try not to vomit. Stick to bland foods that don't trigger it. No salt—we don't want any more swelling. And watch your calories. Managing your weight is also important."

Then, turning to Toots, he asked, "Mrs. Saxe? Millie will need frequent checkups. We need to closely monitor her weight and blood pressure. She's going to need support. If that's too much, we can look into—"

Toots snapped to attention.

"I'm a perfectly capable woman," she growled.

The doctor didn't respond. He moved to a standing desk and began writing appointments in a calendar. Toots hovered behind him, breathing heavy over his shoulder.

When he turned to hand her the carbon copy, his eyes widened and he took a quick step back. Why was Toots standing so close? Millie knew. Her mother was in drill-sergeant mode.

And Millie? She was going to be a grunt in training... *about to march straight into hell.*

~

*BUT A KNIFE. Could she escape hell with a knife?*

Millie stood expressionless in the orange glow of the kitchen nightlight, balancing the blade on her palm. Was she brave enough to use it? Or was there another way?

It had been months since her diagnosis, and she already felt half-dead. Did it matter if she gave up? Her days blurred into an endless cycle of waking up, only to return to bed. She survived on celery sticks and vegetable broth, which left her perpetually hungry. When she tried eating something else, she vomited.

Her life hung by a thread with nobody around to save her. And Toots, who was growing more manic by the month, forbade anybody from trying. Millie later learned that Aunt Mabel, Patrick, and Nellie had tried to visit but were turned away.

It was one of the darkest times of Millie's life.

She pressed the cool, flat blade to her cheek. Holding something so dangerous made her feel powerful, a tool she could use if she wanted.

As a child, when anxiety built up, she sometimes scratched her wrists until they were raw—or once, cut them with a nail file. It drew only a drop of blood. A classmate told the school nurse who in turn referred Millie to a counselor. The counsellor suggested she squeeze or massage something when feeling anxious—like a pillow or stuffed animal—while repeating, *"I'm okay. This feeling will pass. I'm okay. This feeling will pass."*

It had helped then, but not now. Millie wasn't a child anymore, and her adult problems couldn't be fixed by a squeeze or a silly mantra.

Millie carried the knife upstairs, slid it under her mattress, and crawled into bed.

"Oh, Stella," Millie whispered. "I miss your smile, I miss..."

Tears trickled down her cheeks as she stared into the dark, searching for something... anything. "Oh God, I know I've been mad at you for a long time, and maybe I still am. But I'm in a bad, bad place. I don't want to go to hell, but I can't imagine it's worse than this. Please help me. Please tell me what to do."

A clock ticked gently on the nightstand. Across the room, Ginger, her aged hamster and the last of her attic pets, rustled in his shavings. That was it. No angelic choir, no booming voice. Just the silence of a late January evening, followed by the flutter of drooping eyelids and a slow, step-by-step descent into a deeply refreshing sleep.

What a divine gift. After almost seven months of pregnancy, Millie needed all the strength she could get. Doctors had decided her symptoms required inducing labor early.

The procedure was scheduled for the next day.

# CHAPTER 14

## *Back From the Dead*

A loud, mysterious voice boomed, "It's not time yet!"

Millie wasn't sure where it had come from. None of the doctors or nurses surrounding her bed had said it. Their voices sounded more like muffled whispers as they rushed around, frantically hooking up equipment to her perfectly still body.

It wasn't her mother, either. From Millie's vantage point hovering near the ceiling, she saw that Toots wasn't in the room.

Wherever it had come from, Millie wished she hadn't heard it. She was looking down on her body... floating... free... and it was blissfully wonderful.

Until she opened her eyes.

"Mother?" she whispered faintly. Toots was now in the room, talking to a doctor. Everyone else had left. The man placed his hand on Toots's arm, signaling he wanted to speak with Millie first.

"Well, well... how are you doing, young lady?" he asked, approaching her bedside. "You sure gave us a scare. Are you in any pain?"

Millie didn't answer right away. Her brain felt foggy as it struggled to recall the day's events. She remembered feeling faint on the way to the hospital. She recalled being placed on a table, her legs in stirrups, and the searing pain that followed. And standing beside her, a gray-haired nurse shouting, "Breathe, dammit, breathe!"

Everything went dark after that.

"Uhh," Millie rasped. Her throat felt like sandpaper. "I don't know."

That's when it hit her—she'd been pregnant! She tilted her head down to look at her belly, now covered by a sheet. The doctor noticed.

"I'm sorry, Millie. We did everything we could. They didn't make it."

Millie looked up him, cold and stony. The doctor raised an eyebrow in concern.

"Well, we're very glad you're okay," he continued. "You'll need to stay in intensive care for a few days, but then you should be able to return to normal life."

*Normal life? What did that even mean?*

Millie considered telling him about the strange experience she had—but quickly decided against it. It was anything *but* normal, and she really didn't want to see the man raise his other eyebrow.

For the next few days, Millie ate like a starved animal. She growled at the nurses and her mother, devouring everything they brought to her. After months of eating "rabbit food," even the hospital food tasted decadent.

She also tried to process what had happened. She was alive. Her babies weren't. It seemed simple enough. But why didn't she feel more, grief, anger... anything? Was it because she'd spent her entire pregnancy trying not to love her babies, fearing for the lives they might've had?

Sometimes she *had* felt a motherly tug—a flicker of desire to love the lives growing inside her. But doubts always crushed it.

There had been little certainty the twins would survive. She couldn't believe she'd make a good mother. And the idea of peacefully raising children in the same house with Toots had been equally inconceivable.

Then there was the "floating thing" to figure out. How could she have seen herself and the medical team from above? It had been too vivid to just be a dream.

On her last day in the hospital Millie asked the nurse for a phone. Toots hadn't arrived yet, and Millie felt the urge to call Nellie. It had been months since they last spoke and there was so much to catch up on.

The first thing she told her about was the twins. She heard Nellie crying softly on the other end.

"Oh Millie, you must be so heartbroken. I'm so sorry!"

To Millie's surprise, her lip quivered and her eyes welled with tears at the sound of her friend's empathy. She pulled herself together, however, and the feeling passed.

"It is what it is," Millie said flatly, "Life is shitty sometimes, and we have to go on."

She then told Nellie about the floating experience. If anyone would believe her, it would be a friend who already thought she was crazy.

"I've heard of those!" Nellie said excitedly. "Out-of-body experiences I think they're called. That means you died, right?"

"I suppose so. They said my heart stopped briefly, but I don't know for how long."

"Wow, Millie, it's rare to have those. You're so lucky!"

Millie sat up straighter. *Lucky?* That was a word she'd never used to describe herself!

Nellie ended the conversation with an invitation. "When you're out of the hospital and feeling up to visiting, give me a call, okay? I have some news, but I want to tell you in person."

Millie hung up, her breath slowing to a calm, steady rhythm. Her future still felt cloudy, but the sunshine in her friend's voice was something to hold onto.

She could hardly wait to get home... and find out what Nellie's news was.

# CHAPTER 15

## *A Polish Boy*

Nellie shouldered her way through a curtain of wooden beads, carrying a tray of snacks she'd scrounged from the kitchen. Elvis's voice crooned in the background.

"Well, did you like it?" she asked, setting the tray down on the coffee table. "His new song? It's dreamy, right?"

Millie smugly shoved a fistful of stuffing into a pillow she was making for Nellie's sofa. She was pleased with how it was turning out.

"Sure is," Millie said, tapping her chest. "Elvis gets me right in the gills."

Nellie laughed heartily. "Yeah, he gets me there, too—and everywhere else, as well!"

What a ray of sunshine on a cloudy February day: hanging out with a friend listening to music. Only a month had passed since losing the twins, but already Millie was eager to move on with life—any life—that didn't involve locking herself up in the attic. So, when she had heard Nellie and Chuck eloped and moved into a new apartment, she hopped on a bus the next day. Besides, she had a mission. Nellie had always been hopeless when it came to decorating. Over the phone she'd pleaded, *"Please help me groove up my pad. You're so good at it!"*

Millie eyed the snack tray: thick chunks of Velveeta cheese, apple wedges, and Nellie's famous dessert: frozen Ho-Hos snipped with scissors into little rounds. She reached straight for the Ho-Hos.

"So, Nellie," she said, popping one in her mouth, "I didn't know what your surprise was, but wow—marriage? I can't believe it. You seem happy."

She gave the pillow a few firm punches, flipped it, and punched it again. "Perfect. Ready to sew shut."

Nellie handed her the sewing basket. "I *am* happy, Millie. I really think he's the one."

Millie shot her a look.

"Think? Are you *insane,* Nellie? You already tied the knot!"

Nellie's face fell, and Millie immediately felt a stab of guilt. Her friend was doing the best she could. Nothing about her upbringing had been "roses and rainbows" any more than Millie's had. Her mother died when she was five and then her father struggled with a head injury from a trucking accident. Nellie had ended up living with an aunt and uncle who already had too many kids.

Nellie nervously stuffed a chunk of cheese into her mouth and changed the subject. "What about you, Mil'? Any plans this year? Finish school, maybe?"

Millie sighed. "I guess I should get my... what do you call it? GED? I just don't want to go back to school!"

Just then a door slammed, and a bull charged into the room.

The girls jumped. Nellie threw a pillow at him. "Stop coming home like that, Chuck! You scared the bejeebers out of us!"

The man, built like a linebacker, punted the pillow into a corner and bellowed, "Field Goal!"

Then he added, "Did you see the wheels parked outside? It's so cool, man!"

The girls looked at each other and rolled their eyes. Chuck was a man who filled a room with himself *and* his passions: muscle cars and racing. At least those were his current obsessions. He always seemed to be in love with something new every time Millie saw him.

Nellie went to the window.

"Oh, that's Johnny's car," she said, peering down. "You remember him and his brothers, don't you Chuck? The guys from Pennsylvania? I heard Johnny's renting the apartment downstairs."

Chuck remembered. After inhaling half the snack platter, he flew downstairs to talk to Johnny. Before the girls could adjust to his absence, he burst through the door again.

"Johnny and his brothers invited us to their pad! Grab more snacks. I'm bringing my bongos!"

Nellie dashed to the kitchen. Millie thought about stopping her. She wanted to say she wasn't ready for crowds.

But she didn't want to go home, either.

"One hour," she whispered to Nellie as they followed Chuck out the door. "Just *one*, you hear?"

A tall, lanky figure with a mop of blond hair opened the lower apartment door. He grinned widely. "Hey, dude, you made it!"

Then he spotted the girls behind Chuck. "And you brought dudettes! Way cool! Hi, I'm Johnny."

He extended a long arm. "Come in, come in. My pad's humble, but it's yours."

A haze of cigarette smoke filled the room, tinged with patchouli. Johnny gestured toward the kitchen. "The clowns in the kitchen over there, those are my brothers, Stan and Andy."

From behind the counter, two men waved and said hello in unison.

"And that's our other brother, Frank," Johnny added, pointing to a young man with greased black hair and dark-rimmed glasses. Frank, with a guitar on his lap, waved.

A woman walked over and took the platter from Nellie's hands. "Hi, I'm Joanne," she said with a dimpled smile. "I'm Johnny's girlfriend."

"Can you believe this cute little thing is all mine?" Johnny asked, sidling up next to her to highlight their height difference. "Or is she just half mine?"

Joanne wrinkled her nose and laughed, waving toward the living room. "You can sit anywhere you'd like. Just not the beanbag. Andy poked a hole in it... by accident he *says.*"

Andy called from the kitchen. "Yes, by accident, right after Johnny called me the runt of the litter. *Do* remember that little detail!"

Millie took the wingback chair nearest the door. Nellie squeezed herself onto a loveseat with Chuck.

"Just so you know, we're all Polish boys," Stan said, handing out cold beers, "and all we listen to is polka music."

Millie and Nellie raised eyebrows. Even Chuck was speechless. None of them had ever heard polka music before.

"Don't worry, you'll like it," Stan said, walking over to a record player.

For an awkward minute, Millie tried to comprehend the odd, playful tempo she was hearing: a quirky mix of accordion, tuba, and God only knew what else.

The boys broke. One elbowed another, and they all burst out laughing. Andy slapped his knees.

"Ah, we're just teasing you!" Andy said, swapping out the record for a Beach Boys album.

"But not about being Polish!" Stan added with a grin.

Millie started to relax. She pulled her legs into a pretzel and focused on the conversation. This was the first weekend, she learned, that all four of the "Spock boys" were together in Rochester. Their migration had been gradual; Johnny came first, then Frank, followed by Stan. Andy, the youngest, was just visiting. He and their two sisters lived in Pennsylvania near their father.

Millie found herself drawn to Frank, the shy, dark-haired brother seated beside her. He was about her age, but unlike her, skinny as a beanpole. Most of the time, he just picked quietly at his guitar, looking amused at all the bantering going on.

"Hey, Frank," Johnny called, "Tell the girls why you got discharged from the Army!"

Frank rolled his eyes, which Millie thought looked kind.

"Flat feet," he said with a chuckle. "Must've developed them, I guess."

Stan and Andy handed out another round of beers. Millie kept watching Frank. A couple of times—unless she imagined it—he glanced at her over his glasses, smiling shyly before returning to his guitar.

*If he doesn't mean to be adorable,* Millie thought, *he's doing a pretty good job of it.*

A clock on the wall chimed every hour, but Millie didn't hear it the first time... or the second. Something about the Spocks' laid-back conversation put her at ease. There was a politeness, even an amusing innocence, that was refreshingly different.

But as the afternoon light faded and a gentle light snow began to fall, Millie knew she had to get Nellie's attention. Chuck had offered to drive her home so she wouldn't have to take the bus again.

Frank noticed Millie getting ready to leave. He stood, took her coat off a hook, and held it up so she could slip her arms into it. If she hadn't seen the gesture in movies, she might've been confused. It was her first time.

"Would you like to see my new car?" Frank asked as they stepped outside.

Beneath a streetlamp, everyone gathered for one last smoke. Frank walked Millie over to a beige Chevy parked behind Johnny's car. He started it up and blasted the heater. Millie noticed bubbly rust on the wheel wells, covered over with white paint.

"It's not new, actually," Frank admitted sheepishly. "Just my first car."

Millie shivered; her coat wasn't warm enough. Frank noticed.

"Uh-oh, you're cold, aren't you?" he asked. He opened both side doors of his car, creating a little shelter, then gently positioned Millie between them. "Stand here. The wind won't be so harsh."

Millie stiffened; she didn't like anyone "positioning" her.

Frank's face turned red, clearly having meant to be chivalrous.

"S-so, do you live with your mom and dad?" he stammered.

"Yeah, I guess you could say that," Millie replied, then quickly changed the subject. "So, you work here in Rochester?"

"Uh-huh. I'm a butcher's apprentice."

Frank explained how he got the job, moved in with his brother Stan, and adjusted to the culture shock of a big city like Rochester.

"Brady, where I grew up," he continued, "is a very small coal mining town. I don't even remember seeing a police car until I moved here. Now I see them every day!"

It didn't take long for Millie to lower herself onto the edge of the car seat, feeling the heater warm her back. Frank, still standing, fought the wind as it whipped through his slicked-down hair. He kept running his fingers through it.

"What about you?" he asked, uncomfortable with doing most of the talking. "You work somewhere?"

Millie mentioned her job at Fanny Farmer but skipped everything before and after. It was tempting, though. Telling this small-town boy she'd been pregnant, lost twins, and had an out-of-body experience would certainly send him running—which, honestly, she preferred. It would happen sooner or later anyway.

"I like your little cross," Frank said. "Are you religious? I never missed Mass growing up. I was an altar boy. Want to hear some Latin?"

She couldn't help but smile at the funny-sounding words he rattled off.

"No," she said eventually, fingering her cross, "this was just a gift from an aunt. I'm not religious. I'm an atheist."

Millie wasn't really an atheist; she just wanted to see his reaction. Frank looked down, shuffled his boots, then looked up with a mischievous smile.

"So, what would you do," he asked, "if you were stuck at a green light behind a car with one of those bumper stickers that says, 'Honk if you love Jesus'?"

Millie laughed out loud.

"I would convert!" she shot back. This made Frank laugh, too. Millie couldn't believe it. *She said something witty!*

"So, uhh," Frank said, sobering as he noticed Nellie and Chuck approaching. "I enjoyed talking to you, Millie. Would you want to hang out this Saturday? Maybe see a matinee? There's that new drive-in that opened."

Millie felt caught off guard. Nellie was by her side, and Frank's face turned red again. She had to think fast. Frank was a nice guy, but there was no way she wanted him coming to her house.

"Uh, okay" she responded, the words coming out faster than she had wanted. "You can pick me up here at Nellie and Chuck's place. If that's okay with Nellie, that is?"

Nellie grinned and nodded fast.

"Cool, great," Frank said. "I'll be here around noon, then. Well, I'd better hit the road before this snow gets worse."

Millie stood and looked up and down the freshly plowed street. "Well, right now it looks clear as a button!"

Frank smiled. Nellie giggled, and Millie groaned as she watched Frank get into his car and drive off. Did she just say something stupid again?

Maybe even more unsettling... did she *actually* agree to go on a date with a guy?

# CHAPTER 16

# Getting the Blessing

Two bright stars twinkled outside Millie's window, alternating like Morse Code. She thought of her twins— the ones she hadn't named. Usually, it was painful to revisit that memory, but tonight, as she watched the winking stars, she wondered what she would have named them had they lived.

"We have to tell her," Frank said on the phone.

Millie leaned against a pillow on her bed, staring out the window. She fiddled with a ring that now hung with the cross around her neck. It was hard to believe four months had passed since she'd agreed to go out with Frank. Every day since, they'd been hanging out or talking late into the night—a steady, intensifying whirlwind of getting to know each other. And now...

Millie held up the ring, slowly turning it in the moonlight. A tiny diamond sparkled on its delicate silver band. She wasn't wearing it on her hand yet—not wanting her mother to see it—so she kept it close to her heart.

"You haven't changed your mind, have you?" Frank asked, his voice tinged with frustration.

Millie sighed. Why did positive emotions feel so elusive for her?

Even "being in love" seemed more like a means to an end than a feeling to savor and enjoy. Was she worthy of happiness? Wouldn't Frank eventually find her too much to handle?

"Of course not," Millie replied, sharper than intended. "I accepted the ring, didn't I?"

She bit her lip, instantly regretting her tone.

Just a week earlier, Frank had proposed to her. He chose what he thought was a romantic location in Genesee Valley Park—perched together on one of the low-hanging oak tree branches the park was known for. When Frank pulled out the ring, Millie felt both excited and disappointed. They were sitting on the same tree branch where Leo had proposed to Toots!

Summoning courage—not something Millie typically lacked—she said "yes," but not without asking him to propose again somewhere else. Even with an explanation, Frank had looked a little hurt. Meanwhile, a photographer nearby had been looking for a Kodak moment to capture. *Snap!* For a fifty-cent piece from Frank's pocket, the awkward proposal—the only one—was memorialized in a small four-inch square.

Frank fell silent on the phone. Millie started to cry. "I'm a mess, Frank. You have no idea."

"Is there something you haven't told me?" he asked gently. "Because I don't care what it is. Nothing will stop me from wanting to marry you."

"No, that's not it. I think what I'm trying to say is... hold on." Millie set the phone down and blew her nose before returning. "I do love you, Frank. And I want to marry you. It's just that I don't know if I can be a good wife. And I know you want kids, but how do I know if I can—?"

Frank interrupted her. "Listen, hon, I know you're not perfect —neither am I. But we can grow *together*, and we can learn how to be better people *together*. As for kids—it's *you* I want to marry, with or without them. Okay? Please stop worrying about that."

Millie wiped her eyes with the back of her hand. She didn't feel like she deserved this man.

"Okay," she said, exhaling as she looked back up at the sky. The twin stars winked back. "We'll tell my mother this weekend. But you know those boxing gloves in your closet? Bring them, because you're gonna need them!"

THE FOLLOWING SUNDAY, Frank appeared at the front door in a cardigan sweater, thin tie, and his hair slicked back as always. He held out a bouquet of flowers.

"No boxing gloves," he said with a grin. "But maybe these will do?"

Millie gave him a peck. She loved that Frank was old-fashioned and wanted to "get the blessing" of Toots and Leo, even though she still thought it would be easier to elope like Nellie and Chuck did.

"Mother and Leo are on the back porch. Go ahead and sit with them; I'm almost done with the finger sandwiches. Oh, and I made your favorite lemonade. It's already out there."

"Okay. I'll try not to say anything stupid until you get there," he said with a nervous chuckle.

Millie returned to the sandwich platter but kept an eye on the screen door. Leo sat in his usual chair, smoking his pipe in silence. Toots, on the other hand, was standing and giving Frank an education on the proper care and feeding of her porch plants.

*So far, so good,* Millie thought. Still, she sliced and stacked the sandwiches as quickly as possible. Leaving Frank alone was risky. Toots didn't seem to like him; she'd even called him "prudish" once.

And unlike Freddy Flad and a couple of other guys Toots had tried to set her up with, Frank was *Millie's* choice.

Millie nudged the screen door open with her foot and carefully placed the tray on the table.

"Here we are! Oops, I forgot to put the tea kettle on. Would you like some tea, Mom?"

Toots plopped back into her chair and folded her arms.

"Don't bother," she grunted.

*Uh-oh*, Millie thought. *That was a quick change. What did I miss?*

She looked at Frank, who managed a weak smile, then sat on the loveseat beside him.

Toots stared intently at Frank.

"Do you know the poem, *Trees,* by Joyce Kilmer?" she asked.

Frank shook his head.

"Well, I do. I know it by heart."

Toots recited the poem word for word, rocking in her chair without taking her gaze off Frank. Millie fumed. She was doing it again—making sure all the attention stayed on her.

As soon as Toots finished her performance, Millie jumped in. "Mom, I asked Frank to come for lunch because he has something he'd like to ask you and Leo."

Toots leaned back in her chair. "I can see that, you little whore. He can speak for himself. You know how to use that tongue of yours, don't you, Frank?"

She winked, and Frank's eyes widened. He sat up straight, the veins in his neck bulging.

"I don't think that's any way to talk about your daughter," he said, his voice shaking. "I love Millie and she's no whore!"

*Oh boy, this isn't good,* Millie thought. She was used to her mother's trash talk—and knew how to dish it back. This wasn't Frank's world, however. She placed her hand on his knee.

"Let's go," she said firmly.

But it was too late. Toots stood up, her face twisted with anger. She leaned over the coffee table, pointing a finger in Frank's face.

"How dare you tell me how to talk to *my* daughter?" she yelled. "Who do you think you are?"

Millie grabbed Frank's hand.

"Now," she said, pulling him toward the door. She pointed to her mother. "Back off, we're not putting up with this!"

Toots froze for a moment, then stormed around the coffee table. Millie and Frank dashed to the car.

"Quick, floor it!" Millie shouted. Before Frank could fully back out of the driveway, Toots threw herself onto the hood of the car, spread-eagle, gripping the edges.

Frank slammed on the brakes.

"What the hell? Get off my car!" he shouted through the windshield at her furious, frothing face.

Just then Leo—bless his heart—meekly came out and tried to talk Toots down.

Surprisingly, it worked. She slid off, and Frank seized the moment. With a quick prayer that no one was crossing the sidewalk or driving by, he floored it and backed onto the street.

Millie clutched her head, feeling as if it might explode.

"I told you, Frank! You shouldn't have gotten involved with me!"

Frank found a place to pull over. With trembling hands he took Millie's, looking her straight in the eye.

"Listen. I love you. We'll get through this, okay? Let's go to my apartment, have a drink, and unwind."

Millie nodded and looked out the window. Her mother's behavior wasn't surprising, really. It was normal in Millie's world. Growing up, she had even learned most of the local police officers' names. They would often visit to calm Toots down.

But Frank's reaction? *That* wasn't normal. He confronted her mother's foul mouth! He defended Millie! No one had ever stood up for her like that. No one had ever tried to protect her sexual purity—not that there was any left to protect. Frank knew about the abuse, the twins, and most of her past... at least the important parts. And still, he loved her.

"I don't deserve you," she said for the hundredth time. "I really don't."

As night fell, Frank pleaded with her to stay at his apartment where she'd be safe. He even suggested they elope now. But Millie insisted he take her back home. She had plenty of experience navigating Toots's moods, and the consequences would be worse if she didn't go back.

When Millie walked through the door, she found Toots lying on the couch with a wet rag on her forehead. Her face was blotchy and tear-streaked, and crumpled tissues littered the floor around her. Behind her, the kitchen was a mess, and the platter of sandwiches still sat on the porch table.

"I'm home," Millie said.

"Leave me alone," Toots said in a quivering voice. "I'm a rotten person. *Rotten, rotten, rotten!*"

Millie sat on the edge of Leo's chair—a safe distance from the couch.

"I mean it," Toots continued, her voice breaking with pitiful, childlike sobs. "I'm a terrible person, and you don't love me. *Nobody* loves me!"

"Listen to me, Mother," Millie said wearily. "You're not a terrible person, and I do love you. But you need to understand that I love Frank, too, and I'm going to marry him—with or without your blessing. We're going to live together and hopefully start a family together. I'm old enough to make this decision on my own."

Toots removed the rag from her forehead and blinked rapidly at the ceiling.

"Now," Millie said, standing up. "I'm going to tidy the kitchen up a bit and then go to bed. I'm exhausted."

"I'll take you to see Dr. Sloan this week."

Millie cocked her head. "What for?"

"You have to be tested for syphilis and measles to get a marriage license," Toots said, sitting up straighter. "And he needs to check you over to see if you're healthy enough for another baby."

Millie left for the kitchen, feeling uneasy why Toots had shifted her tone so quickly. Was it because she was firm with her? Or because she mentioned starting a family?

*It doesn't matter,* she thought as she hurried to wash the dishes. *Our children will belong to us, and we'll live far away in a house in the country with a dog and a garden and—*

Millie placed the last dish in the drying rack and pulled the sink plug. As the water drained out, so did her dreams.

*Damn, I can't even afford a doctor's appointment without Toots's help! How will Frank and I ever save enough money to move out of the city? Frank's pay isn't enough. And we can't ask Frank's father for anything; he's on a limited income.*

Her chest tightened. Why did life always feel so out of her control? Would she have to depend on Toots and Leo forever?

*One thing is certain,* Millie resolved as she ascended the stairs. *This marriage thing has to work!*

# CHAPTER 17

# Goodbye Dolly

Millie didn't know many Bible verses, but her Aunt Ethel had made one of them unforgettable: "*When I was a child, I acted like a child, but when I became an adult, I put away childish things.*"

Ethel wielded this verse like a Wiffle bat, quoting it at Harvey whenever he retreated to the garage on Saturday afternoons to watch professional wrestling on his little black-and-white television. Harvey, however, had mastered the art of duck-and-cover. He would stay out there even longer, filling it with the smell of his "stinky sticks," as Ethel called his cigars, until she eventually missed him and called him inside for lemon meringue pie.

Somehow, their marriage had endured longer than anyone in the family.

Thinking about this memory, Millie walked around her bedroom, stopping to brush away the cobwebs that covered her old hobby horse like a forgotten museum relic. She was suddenly feeling nostalgic about so many things: Aunt Ethel, Patrick, the softball team... even her childhood toy.

"Can you believe it, Dolly?" she asked it. "Can you believe I'm a married woman now?"

A suitcase lay behind her on the bed, along with a large box containing a white silk dress edged with lace. Toots had agreed to store the wedding dress in the attic. She also told Millie she'd keep the attic furnished... "just in case you and Frank have a fight and you want to move back home."

Millie fumed. What an inappropriate thing to say at her wedding reception! Even if she and Frank had problems, she wouldn't go crying to Toots. So what if she and Frank were dirt poor, only able to afford an apartment barely bigger than the attic? So what if Frank sometimes drank too much and she still struggled with anger and depression? Love would carry them through anything, right?

Millie took a deep breath and smoothed down the new plaid poncho she was wearing. Her stomach felt flatter than usual under the poncho, which made her feel good, but it was churning with nerves. She had spent most of her nineteen years in this dismal attic. Shouldn't she be more excited to leave?

The voices of Frank, Toots, and a few lingering guests—including Nellie and Chuck—drifted up the stairs. Patrick and his boyfriend had left early to take Aunt Mabel home. How nice it had been to see her aunt on this special day! Toots still held a grudge against her, but she dropped it long enough to keep the wedding, and even the reception, mostly drama-free.

In fact, Toots had been on her best behavior since her last episode. While still opinionated, she had been helpful, even contributing generously to the wedding costs. The biggest hurdle had been deciding where the wedding would take place. Toots had wanted it to be at the nearby Methodist church where she was a member, but Frank's pick was Rochester's Saint Josaphat Ukrainian Catholic Church.

It had been a no contest. Toots begrudgingly backed down when Millie reminded her that Frank had never missed a Sunday Mass in his entire life.

"Honey!" Toots called up the stairs, adding a cackle. "You and Frank need to drive Chuck and Nellie home! They drank too much!"

"Not me, I'm good!" shouted Nellie, her voice ending in a loud, masculine belch.

"You're cut off, Nellie!" Millie yelled down the stairs. "Mom! Would you tell Frank to come up here and help me with the suitcase?"

Millie paused at her window to close it, shutting out the early evening air along with the familiar chatter of car horns, voices in the street, and two dogs barking back and forth. Oh, how often she had leaned on that ledge to dream, cry, and pray to God! From this spot she had longed for stability and truth. She had longed for siblings. She had longed to die. And she had longed to live.

She went to sit on the bed and wait for Frank.

"I'm coming, my lady in the tower!" Frank shouted as he bounded up the stairs. "I'm coming to rescue you!"

He walked in to find his princess brooding.

"Hey, you okay? Your mother didn't mean to crush your center-piece, you know. It was an accident."

"Yeah, I know. But I did spend $20 of our money on supplies to make it!" she said, frowning. "Are you sure I shouldn't get a job, Frank? What if the other shoe will kick? What if I get pregnant before we're ready for—"

Frank, sitting beside Millie, gently pressed a finger to her lips to hush her—a surprisingly bold move that she didn't want him to do again.

"Do you mean," he asked, "'what if the other shoe drops?' Seriously, hon, you're worrying about finances on our honeymoon? I told you, I want to take care of you. I don't want my wife working if I'm perfectly capable of doing it myself. Come on, don't ruin our night."

Millie stood and sighed. Frank was a good man; it was time to tuck her worries away for another day. They were on their way to Niagara Falls—a modest choice, but an adventure all the same.

She surveyed the attic one last time. Except for her old dog Ladybug—who Millie decided should stay with Toots—everything important to her was already at Millie and Frank's new apartment, or packed in the bulging suitcase on the bed.

"I almost missed this," she said, suddenly spotting something she had forgotten.

She unpinned a metal button from the window curtain and tossed it onto the bed. "Slip that into the suitcase, would you? But don't unzip it all the way. It'll explode!"

"I'm OK, God Doesn't Make Junk." Frank read from the button. "Where'd you get this?"

"A stranger gave it to me when I was little. I found it recently."

"Cool. Oh, your mother said something weird downstairs. She called our apartment a stupid little shoebox, and said she's 'doing something about it.' Do you know what she's talking about?"

Millie swallowed hard; she didn't know Toots would move that fast.

"Uh, she's working with a realtor friend to get a certain house for us."

"A house? Where?"

"On Hazelwood Terrace. The owners are supposedly moving into a retirement home."

Frank's eyes widened. "So close to your mother? No way, Millie. We're trying to get away from her—not live in the same neighborhood! Besides, we don't have a down payment for a house."

"She said she'll give us the money for it."

"Absolutely not," Frank said adamantly, his eyes flashing. "I won't be indebted to her. You know how she—"

"Stop," Millie interrupted, turning off the lamp and heading toward the stairs. "Whose turn is it now to be a worrywart? It'll all work out."

Frank grabbed the suitcase and followed Millie, his face solemn. He said nothing more. Would it all work out? He hoped to God it would.

# CHAPTER 18

# The Last Straw

Using a sewing machine had always been Toots's forte, but watching Millie, you wouldn't guess she was a newbie. The patchwork material under the pounding needle advanced at a smooth, rhythmic pace, and her foot held steady pressure on the pedal. After seven years of marriage, she gained at least a few new skills. Making curtains, however, was easier than the challenge of being a wife and mother. When it came to that, Millie felt deeply unprepared and constantly on edge.

"Done," she said, stopping to wipe her brow. She lifted the needle lever and removed the material. "I can finally return this machine to Mom."

It was an ambitious project to take on—curtains for the whole house—but a necessary one. Rochester was still reeling from the "Alphabet Murders," a series of three brutal child murders between 1971 and 1973. The tragedy had even struck the family of Millie's own sister-in-law, and the monster was still out there. Heavy, light-blocking curtains was hardly protection, but Millie couldn't stand the thought of anyone seeing her kids through the windows at night.

Grabbing a handful of hooks that Toots had given her, Millie stood on tiptoe to hang her newly-made curtains in the big bay window. Then she stepped back. They were cheerful enough, she'd give them that, but if money weren't so tight she would've preferred to tear out the dingy brown paneling, rip up the hideous orange shag carpet, and buy store-bought curtains instead.

Not that she complained much about the house. Frank did enough of that for the both of them. He was still upset that Toots had provided the down payment for it... and that they lived only a few streets apart.

But what choice did they have? They hadn't expected to have two children so early in their marriage. And if not for Toots, they'd still be stuck in that cramped, "shoebox" apartment. Their new house was small, close to the road, but it was still a *house*—with a backyard, a clothesline, and even a front porch.

*If only Frank made more money, we wouldn't need my mother,* Millie thought. *Then we could move to the country instead of just dreaming about it!*

The grandfather clock—another gift from Toots—chimed four times. It was time to check on the kids. Millie peeked through their door. Shy, sweet Pamela, born on Leo's birthday, was now six years old. She had thrown off the covers, her wispy blonde hair clinging in ringlets around her angelic face. Millie felt immense relief when Pamela's chickenpox fever had broken earlier that morning. Her worry almost rivaled the anxious nights she had spent pacing the apartment while Frank worked nights, imagining every worst-case scenario. She had feared that Pamela would share the same fate as the twins. That she would fail as a mother. That she would feed her baby too little, or—as had been done to her—*too much.*

Then there was little Frankie Jr., born a year and a half later. His fever, which had been less severe, broke first. What a happy, easy-to-laugh baby he had been compared to Pamela. Maybe it was because by then, Millie had become more relaxed as a mother—at least in knowing she could have another healthy pregnancy.

Still, motherhood felt unnatural to Millie. Even Nellie, who also had two young children, seemed to handle it better.

"Don't worry so much," her friend had said to her one day. "We can't *all* be a June Cleaver."

Millie left their bedroom door open and went to check on her homemade chicken noodle soup. The kids didn't like it—except the noodles—but she always made it when they were sick.

She heard a car door shut outside.

"I'm home!" Frank called as he entered. He let the screen door slam and tossed his briefcase on the couch. He had just been trained for a sales position at Farrel's, a plastic injection mold company. It was only commission-based to start, but he was glad his job didn't involve gutting animals or handling dangerous factory machines anymore.

"Shush! The kids are still napping," Millie snapped through the kitchen pass-through. "And stop slamming that door! You're going to loosen it off its hinge again!"

"Uh-oh, did you talk to your mother today?" Frank joked. Then, seeing the look on her face, he quickly changed the subject. "How are the kids?"

"Pam's fever broke. Frankie's fine."

Millie hovered over the soup, feeling too sad to meet Frank's gaze. She didn't want to be in a bad mood every time he came home.

"I'm sorry," Frank said. He wrapped his arms around her waist from behind. "It's not easy to deal with sick kids all day."

"I've been so emotional lately," she whimpered. Frank rested his chin on her shoulder.

"Do you miss Leo?" he asked, gently rocking her. "I know you loved him."

Millie stirred the soup. Her heart was still heavy having found

Leo sitting in his armchair, his head slumped over, with tobacco pipe still in hand. Fortunately, Frank had been with her. Amidst Toots's frantic cries in the background, he had even tried, clumsily yet valiantly, to resuscitate him. But it had been too late. They had to say goodbye to the quiet, gentle man who was the only father Millie had ever known.

"Yes, I miss him," Millie said. "He didn't have a mean bone in his body."

Frank picked up an apple from the fruit bowl. "Is your mother still acting nutsy? I worry every time you go over there, you know."

"I can handle her," Millie answered, trying to sound convincing. Although the truth was, Toots's mental health had declined since Leo passed away, and she was even starting to bring men to the house again. "I don't stay there long, and I never leave the kids alone with her anymore."

"Good," Frank said. "We can always find another babysitter."

Millie pursed her lips. They couldn't afford a babysitter! Every spare dollar was socked away to buy a house in the country. Until Frank got a salary position—or a second job—Millie was the cook, bottle washer, *and* babysitter. And if her mother didn't occasionally slip her money she wouldn't even have a bottle to wash!

"What's this?" Frank asked, picking up an envelope from the table. "Is this what I think it is?"

"Yeah, they don't have any record of her. We shouldn't have wasted money on that. But you talked me into it."

"I thought it was important for you to find your birth mother."

Millie didn't say anything.

"Well, I have good news," Frank said, changing the subject again. He sat down at the table. "Johnny found an engine for me to put into the Chevy."

"I still don't know why we can't use Leo's old car."

"I told you. That thing will cost more to fix than putting a new engine in ours."

"You're biting off more than you can chew. You need to get another job."

"You're nagging again. Don't you think I'm trying?"

"Has that other company contacted you yet?"

"If I hear from them, I'll tell you."

"It's been too long. Call them."

Frank shoved his chair away from the table. It was starting; they were about to have another fight over money.

Millie stood with her arms folded. Frank was living in a fantasy world. Every weekend for the last year, they'd been driving out to the country to look for land. How long would this go on? Forever? They were stuck in a rut, and someone—not her—seemed content to stay there.

Frank spun around angrily, grabbed a six-pack from the fridge, and headed for the cellar, slamming the door behind him. It was a partially finished space, mostly used as a playroom for the kids. It was also his "man cave" when Millie was in one of her moods.

Left alone in the kitchen, Millie pressed her hands to her eyes.

"Oh God!" she cried, for what felt like the hundredth time that week. Anxiety squeezed her chest like a vise. She was horrified to admit it, but sometimes suicide crossed her mind. A dark thought—one she had the immediate sense to quash—but it still lingered in her subconscious like a shadow, waiting for her to entertain it.

Five chimes from the clock. Millie grabbed the envelope off the table and crammed it into the trash. Time to get dinner on the table —*again.*

❧

AUTUMN CAME A FEW MONTHS LATER, bringing a brisk change in the air. Was it for better or worse? Millie couldn't say. She just knew *something* was stirring.

One Sunday morning, she pulled three coats from the closet and said to Frank, "I'm going to my mother's. The kids want to give her the paper mâché animals they made in Sunday school. I won't be long."

Frank winced as he wedged a screwdriver under a jammed window frame. The repairs on their old house never seemed to end. "Do you want to go to the land when you get back? It's a beautiful day."

Millie didn't answer right away. Finally, after years of scraping and skimping, they had bought a single acre in Walworth, New York —a cornfield kind of town where the sun sets between houses and curtains weren't even necessary! She did like taking the forty-minute trip out there to mow, plan their future home, and plant little trees, but now the struggle was to come up with a down payment to get the builder started.

"I'll see how I feel when I get back," she said, heading out the door. Maybe Toots would slip her a few bucks? While Millie knew she didn't visit her for that reason, it was hard not to appreciate the extra pocket money.

At the car, Millie buckled Frankie in. "Hurry up, Pam. We don't have all day."

Pamela was lost in her imagination, circling the yard with her new favorite toy: a stiff collar and leash that gave the illusion of walking an invisible dog.

"Don't drag it behind you," Millie said. "You're getting it dirty."

Millie snatched the leash from Pamela's hand and held it out in front of her. "See? Like this. This is how you hold it."

Pamela's face fell, and she bent down to pat her invisible dog's head.

Just then, Millie felt that all-too-familiar stab of guilt. She was doing it again... snapping at the kids over nothing. The week before, when they'd spilled a box of crayons on the rug, she'd totally lost control—screaming, even swearing—until Pamela ran and hid in her room, and Frankie, wide-eyed and trembling, stayed behind to clean up the mess alone.

"Here," Millie said to Pamela after she crawled into the car with her leash. "You can hold the animals. Just don't crush them."

Pamela reached for the paper bag that held a dove, a sheep, and Frankie's odd interpretation of a camel.

"Can we get an ice-cweam cone?" Frankie asked as they pulled out of the driveway.

"No," Millie said. "Gramma will have cookies."

When they reached Toots's house, Millie turned off the engine and noticed her mother's rose bushes. They looked sickly and over-grown with weeds. Toots hadn't been taking care of her yard lately.

Millie spotted laundry on the clothesline.

"Good, she's home," she said, knowing Toots had a phobia about leaving the house with clothes on the line, convinced the neighbors would steal them.

Pamela and Frankie unbuckled themselves and raced to Gram-ma's back porch, where Ladybug's dog bowl sat. Though the family dog had died a few years back, Toots used his bowl for her outside cat. The kids grabbed some kibble and ran to the fence that bordered old Sal's yard.

"Popeye, Olive Oyl!" they called out, peering through the fence's knotholes. Sal's two Saint Bernards—a brother and sister—rushed to gobble the treats the kids were popping through the holes.

Meanwhile, Millie started taking laundry off the line. The back door slammed.

"What the hell are you doing?" Toots yelled, storming down the steps. "I just hung those up. They're still wet!"

"No, they're bone dry," Millie replied.

Toots didn't hear her—or chose not to. She marched over, yanked the basket from Millie's hands, and scattered the clothes across the lawn.

Frankie squealed with delight and ran over to play in them.

"No!" Millie yelled, trying to pull the clothes out of Frankie's hands. He refused to let go. Millie slapped his hand, and he let out a blood-curdling scream.

"See what you did!" Toots shouted. "Just stop it, will you? You're an insane, incompetent mother!"

Toots plopped onto the grass beside Frankie, bad knees and all, and pulled a towel over her head. Then she peeked out puckered her lips like a fish until Frankie laughed.

That's when, in a moment of clarity, Frank flashed into Millie's mind... calm, protective Frank. She knew what she had to do.

Grabbing both children by the hands, she led them to the car.

"I won't be bringing the kids over here anymore," she said, calm yet firm.

Toots managed to push herself up and hobbled after them. "Over my dead body! You can't keep me from seeing *my* grand-children!"

Millie turned. "Listen, Mom, you can't badmouth me in front of the kids. I won't put up with it anymore."

"Don't you tell me what I can and cannot do!" Toots yelled. "You don't scare me. I have a lawyer. I can get those kids taken away from you, and you wouldn't be able to stop me!"

Upon returning home, Millie told Frank everything. His face tensed with every detail.

"I'm proud of you for standing up to her," he said. "But now we need to talk about her threat. What if she tries to take the kids? I'm not comfortable with us seeing her anymore."

Millie nodded in agreement, although she was certain Toots

couldn't pull off such a stunt in her physical and mental condition. What concerned Millie more were the implications of cutting her out of their lives. As consumed as Toots could be by momentary rages, she was equally prone to extreme remorse—often accompanied by days of crying and suicide threats.

Frank looked at his watch and asked, "It's almost lunch. Do you want to pack sandwiches and have a picnic at the land? We can talk more on the way."

"Yes!" Millie said, springing up. "There's so much to discuss!"

Just before reaching the kitchen, she stopped and spun around. A fierce energy surged through her, like a mother bear defending her cubs.

"Let's do something else, Frank! Let's get that loan and give the builder the go-ahead to start the house as soon as possible, before the ground freezes. Then we can start getting this house ready for sale."

Frank raised an eyebrow. "Are you sure? I thought you wanted to wait until we had more money saved up."

"I don't want to wait any longer!" Millie said, her voice rising. "It's time to get this ball on the road!"

# CHAPTER 19

# Love Notes

Overstuffed junk drawers that were nearly impossible to open. Plastic bags filled with forgotten odds and ends under the bed. Millie couldn't call herself an organizer, per se, but on most days, she didn't consider herself "messy," either. The visible parts of her home were always tidy and inviting. As for filing and storing small things like paperwork, she didn't agree with others that her method was "chaos." Even though she never seemed to be able to find an important receipt or piece of mail, it was rarely her fault. It was usually somebody else who lost it... before she had the chance to lose it herself.

On more realistic days, however, things were different. Finally taking responsibility for her messes, Millie would go into attack mode, slashing and sorting through the clutter until the job was done.

One such day came in the summer of 1977. It was two years after their decision to accelerate the build of their country home, and about a year after they'd moved in. On the surface, life was good. Frank was doing well at his sales job, which now paid a steady salary. Toots had sold her house and moved to Florida to live with a man she'd met. And Millie's home—still carrying that "new house smell"—was decorated and cozy, just how she liked it.

The bedroom closet, however, was a rainy-day project that could no longer wait for rain.

Millie looked for Frank, spotting him in the backyard.

"Hey, up here!" she called down from the bedroom window. "What are you doing? I could use some help!"

Frank was walking from the shed carrying a bag of tools. He squinted up at her.

"I'm trying to fix the mower," he said, wiping sweat off his brow. "It was nice of Stan to give it to us, but I still can't get it to start."

"The air filter could be dirty," Millie said.

"I replaced that already," Frank said in a patient tone. Some men would have been offended by their wife offering advice on something she didn't know how to use—let alone fix—but Frank's pride didn't lean that way. He knew he could overlook a basic solution now and then.

"The closet in here is driving me crazy," Millie said. "You need to find another place for your guitars. They can't stay in there."

"Okay, I'll be up shortly."

Behind Frank, in the alfalfa field, Millie saw Pamela and Frankie playing *Cops and Robbers* with Doug and Debra Weeks, the neighbor kids who lived a quarter mile down the road. They were the same ages as Pamela and Frankie—a double-match made in heaven. Pamela and Debra were struggling to tie Doug up with a rope, while Frankie was slowly running toward them, arms pumping like the Bionic Man.

"I'm coming to save you, Doug!" Frankie shouted.

Millie's gaze drifted to the row of trees beyond the field, their leaves glistening beneath the moving clouds. She still couldn't believe it sometimes—this *new* view from her *new* window. No ugly apartment buildings. No barking dogs or blaring music. No more worrying about her kids playing outside.

And yet, despite all her blessings, Millie's mood was sour. It didn't match the gratitude she felt, or thought she should feel, which only confused her more.

Did she miss Toots? Sometimes she thought so. The boundary she and Frank had drawn for their kid's protection, and their overall sanity, hadn't been meant to shut her out completely. It was just unfortunate that it had come to that. In the two times they'd heard from Toots in the last year and a half, she seemed oblivious to the role her actions had played in their rift.

Maybe what discouraged Millie most was the absence of family. Aside from Frank and the kids, and the occasional check-in with Nellie, she had no one. No friends. No blood relatives. She felt like a nobody.

Millie turned to the closet and with jerky, harried movements began dragging out boxes and riffling through them. A manila envelope with a large heart drawn on the front caught her attention. Sitting on the edge of the bed, she placed it her lap.

*Wow, I haven't seen these in a while,* she thought, reaching inside and pulling out a handful of notes: some scribbled on company memo paper, other on time punch cards and napkins.

Back when they were newlyweds, and Frank worked second shift, he had the romantic habit of writing her notes at work and tucking them in his lunchbox for her to find the next morning when she packed it again.

She had almost forgotten she'd saved them!

The top note read:

*"I miss you so terribly when I'm at work, I can hardly stand it. Do you feel the same way, my darling? Every day I pinch myself that you're my wife."*

Beneath it was another, written when she was pregnant with Pamela:

"*Can you believe we're going to have a baby girl? I'm so proud of you, I could just burst! It's going to be so grand. I'm already in love with our little Pamela.*"

There were even a few notes from Millie to Frank, though not as many.

One read: "*My dear Frank, I love you so much. You're so good to me. I don't deserve your love.*"

And another: "*I'm sorry I snapped at you yesterday. I don't know how you can love a mess like me.*"

Millie's brow furrowed. Still clutching the notes, her hands slowly dropped to her sides. It struck her how different her expressions were from Frank's. She sounded like an immature girl with a terrible self-image.

Now thirty, why did it feel she hadn't grown up?

Frank walked into the bedroom.

"Where do you want me to put my guitars?" he asked. "I can put them in the heated part of the basement for now."

Millie quickly stuffed the notes—and her emotions—back into the envelope.

"Oh, good," she said, pulling a pile of clothing off the guitar cases. "Thanks, I'm just so frustrated today."

Frank leaned against the dresser and noticed a pamphlet lying where he'd left it, a brochure for a weekend conference called *Marriage Encounter*.

"Have you given any thought to this yet?" he asked, holding it up.

"Not yet," Millie said. "Please just take these. I'm tired and I don't have time to talk."

Frank walked out with his guitars, feeling discouraged himself.

After the kids were in bed, Millie and Frank sat in their patio chairs on the back porch. They didn't say much at first; just listened to the chorus of crickets and frogs fill the evening air from a small pond in the distance.

Frank decided to bring up Millie's temper. It had been getting to him more than usual.

"I know," she said with a sigh. "I don't know why I'm like that. I feel sad inside, and then it comes out, I guess, as anger."

Millie sighed again.

"I'm discouraged about my weight, too." She pinched her stomach. "Look. I have three love handles now."

Frank exhaled in frustration. "I wish you'd stop saying those things. You know I don't care about that. If it bothers you that much, then lose the weight."

To Frank's relief, Millie didn't seem to hear him. She continued. "My mother overfed me, you know, when I was a baby. She was grooming me into a mini her. I would never do that to my kids."

Frank pressed his lips together. He wanted to help Millie sort out her feelings, especially when she seemed willing to talk about them. It always felt like a losing battle, though. Whenever she acted like Toots, she didn't see it, and even if she did, she didn't change. After shedding some apologetic tears, she'd explode again in a few days like a pressure cooker without a release valve.

Besides, Frank wasn't a therapist; he had his own issues.

"I get it, I guess," Frank said, picking at a hangnail. "The sadness part. I feel it whenever we fight. And when we... well, you know, when we're not close. Maybe that's why I drink. Some things are ingrained in us from childhood, I guess."

Millie pulled a thin blanket around her shoulders, tucking it under her chin. She watched Frank chew on his nail. She rarely thought of her "nice" husband as "sad"—though he certainly had memories that haunted him.

When he was twelve, his mother died of a mysterious stroke-like illness, and his father, a factory worker, was left to raise six kids on a shoestring budget. Broken in spirit and dulled by the bottle, his father had a particularly bad night when he yelled down the stairs, "It's all your fault your mother died so young!"

Although Frank's siblings had been present—each of them knowing their father wasn't in his right mind—Frank believed his father had looked straight at him when he said those words.

From that day on, Frank had carried a burden of guilt and rejection.

"I still wish you wouldn't drink," Millie said tersely, not wanting her empathy for Frank to cloud her judgment. Sometimes she felt he used his father's drinking as an excuse for his own.

Frank shrugged. "I don't know how to change any more than you do. I mean, *really*, Millie. We live in a beautiful new house. We go to Mass every week. We even do regular confessions. All this stuff should be working."

It was Millie's turn to tighten her lips. Following Catholic tradition was Frank's thing. While she *was* interested in learning about God and Jesus, she found the rituals lifeless. Most of the people seemed more eager to leave church than to arrive. What was appealing about going, if it was only to go through the motions?

Frank slapped at a mosquito on his arm and pointed to a brochure resting on a plant stand in front of them. "I see you brought that out here. What do you think? Any interest? Maybe it'll help our marriage?"

"I don't know," she said, her voice hesitant. She reached to pick it up.

Frank read her mind. "I know it's probably more religious than you like, but Sam and Bernie seemed to enjoy it. At least think about it for, you know..."

He hesitated before finishing. "You know. For Bernie's sake."

Millie bit her lip. She was still emotional about her friend's recent death.

"You two had a connection," he said, "like two peas in a pod."

Frank got up and started toward the door. "Think about it. I'll be right back. Can I get you anything? One of those cookies?"

Millie nodded. "And a small glass of milk, too."

With Frank inside, Millie's mind wandered back a few months. Sam and Bernie were friends they had gotten to know at the Catholic church. To Millie, Bernie was a *real* Christian: free of prudish self-righteousness or fake smiles. She had a humble faith and a sparkling outlook on the afterlife. Even after being diagnosed with cancer and lying on her deathbed, her exuberance never faded.

"I can see, Millie! I can see!" she gasped with one of her final breaths.

Then, as her eyes locked onto something beyond the hospital wall, Millie witnessed a moment she'd never forget. Her friend's face was glowing like a morning glory reflecting the sun's rays.

"I still don't understand it," Millie said to Frank as he returned through the sliding glass doors, balancing a tray with cookies and milk. He placed it on the stand.

"Understand what?" he asked, taking a cookie.

"How I saw what I did, but Sam said I wasn't in the room when Bernie died. It felt so real to me."

"We talked about that; it had to have been a vision. You seem to have a gift for stuff like that. Even Sam thinks so."

Millie fidgeted with the brochure before spreading it open in her lap. She remembered her out-of-body experience when her heart stopped, and the "beings" she used to see in the attic. These weren't even half of the strange things she had seen and experienced. But a gift? Somehow, that didn't encourage her. *What good is a gift if you don't know how to use it?*

"This is good," Millie said, reading the back page. "They have a daycare camp for kids on the same grounds."

"Then it's settled? I need to know, so I can give my boss advance notice."

Millie leaned back and closed her eyes. She didn't know if the conference would help, but she needed to try something. She wanted what Bernie had. And she really did want to be a better wife and mother.

"All right, Frank," she finally said. "We can try it out."

Frank slapped at another mosquito and stood up. He grabbed his glass of milk. "I've got to go in. These things are monsters tonight. I'll tell my boss tomorrow."

"Oh, by the way," he said, pausing at the door. "The conference is in Syracuse. You'd have time to stop at the Vital Records building."

Millie stayed outside for a while, nibbling her cookie and thinking about Frank's comment. With the move and everything else, she'd nearly forgotten about searching for her birth mother. Frank had even suggested an alternative spelling of Jeanette Coyer... but still, it hadn't felt like a priority.

Maybe before looking for somebody else, she should find herself first?

# CHAPTER 20

# The Heat Is On

I t had to be at least ninety degrees inside the crowded auditorium. Most women fanned themselves with brochures, but Millie used an entire Bible. All the while, her thoughts were far from sacred.

*Who's in charge of this conference? It's like a sardine can in here! Didn't they test the air conditioning first?*

On stage, nearly dwarfed by a podium, a skinny wisp of a woman shared an emotional story about her daughter's death and its effect on her marriage. Her husband, broader but with a thin, droopy face, stood beside her and repeatedly caressed her bony back.

Millie shifted uncomfortably in the pew. It was the second day of the marriage conference, and so far, she was disappointed with it. The romance had been snuffed out before they even arrived! The kids, initially excited about going to a Bible camp with games and crafts, suddenly began whining as they packed. Frank, missing his exit for Syracuse, added twenty tense minutes to their already stressful ride. Then, to top it all off, their stop at the Vital Records office had been another waste of time.

The woman finished her story, and her husband took over.

After nervously clearing his throat into the microphone, he forced a toothy smile.

"I'm here to tell you something important," he declared loudly, his gestures out of sync with his words. "We are living testimonies that marriages can be turned around with the power of prayer!"

Millie tried not to roll her eyes. Instead, she focused on the Styrofoam cup in her hands, swirling the last bit of lukewarm ginger ale at the bottom. Frank's arm draped across her shoulders—a gesture many men used with their wives—felt heavy and controlling.

*Why am I so critical?* she asked herself. *Don't I believe in the power of prayer?*

Maybe not. If she was honest, God felt distant—like Leo had been—too weak and broken to stand up for himself or her. No, Millie reasoned, prayer might work for others, but she had to fend for herself. Even though Frank was a good husband, she saw him as weak, too. In fact, all men were weak, and the only way to survive in the world was for her to be strong.

Disturbed by these thoughts, Millie handed her cup to Frank and twisted her neck to check the clock on the wall. She desperately needed air.

It was nearly noon. She sighed and leaned back. Only a few more minutes to sweat it out before lunch.

AT THE FAR end of the cafeteria, Millie saw Frank waving to her. She was leaving the buffet bar, balancing an overloaded tray. When she reached the table, she carefully set the tray down, allowing Frank to push in her chair. He gave her a gentle squeeze on the shoulder before sitting down himself.

Frank had earlier chosen a table near the air conditioner, at

Millie's insistence, and it was filling up fast. Across from them sat a gray-haired couple who introduced themselves as "Sarge and Marge" —names easy to remember because Sarge was bald, and Marge was noticeably large. They had been married for thirty years and attended the conference whenever it came to Western New York.

"We've done it seven or eight times," Marge said, her face beaming.

"Why?" Millie asked. She was surprised that anyone would attend it more than once. "Isn't it supposed to help marriages?"

For a moment both Sarge and Marge looked like they'd swallowed a fireball. Even Frank turned red—but Marge quickly recovered.

"It does help our marriage, I think," she said, nudging Sarge playfully with her elbow. "But mostly, it's the people we come for— meeting new friends, encouraging people. It's fun."

Sarge nodded in agreement. Then Marge cupped her hand and leaned forward to say something just for Millie.

"I can't bear children," she whispered, "so I struggle with loneliness sometimes. You young folks make our hearts sing."

Millie set her fork down, her chewing slowing to a stop. An older, childless woman struggling with loneliness but choosing to give back to others? This touched Millie on a deep level.

On the other side of Frank, a woman in her fifties sat alone. Her jet-black hair was neatly coiffed around a pale chiseled face perched upon a giraffe-like neck. A crisp, buttoned-up white shirt with a large brooch completed her regal look. Millie kept trying to recall where she had seen her before.

The woman introduced herself to Sarge, who sat diagonally across from her.

"My name is Nadine Nordstrom," she said, reaching a delicate hand across the table to shake his. Even the cadence of her voice seemed familiar.

Then it clicked. *Stella!* The black hair in a bun, the large brooch, the formal yet friendly voice... they were all features that reminded her of her old boss at the candy factory!

As lunch wound down, Millie pulled the schedule from her purse. She knew she had to decide quickly; the afternoon was about to begin with its array of "break-out" sessions.

"So, what did you kids pick out for your next class?" Marge asked.

Millie signaled to Frank to let him answer first. He informed Marge that he had decided on a men's only class. Millie was still debating. What she *really* wanted to do was nap, but that was out of the question. The dorm rooms didn't have air conditioning!

She looked down at the list again. That's when she noticed a class being taught by Nadine. It was titled *A Family Foundation: How to Build on a Relationship with God.* It was something in the description itself, however, that sparked her interest: words like "nonreligious," and "this content might be slightly controversial."

*What's not to like already?*

Millie tapped the paper.

"This one," she said. "This one interests me."

# CHAPTER 21

# Seed on Good Soil

Every room along the hall seemed hushed—except Room 153.

Millie walked through its door to discover that the music was coming from a tape deck next to Nadine, and the laughter from some gregarious people who had arrived early.

Millie chose a chair at the end of the long rectangular table. The room quickly filled up.

Nadine finally looked at her watch and turned off the music. "Welcome, everyone," she said cheerfully, waiting for the chatter to die down. "My name is Nadine Nordstrom, and I'm glad to see you all here today. Before we begin, I'd like to offer a brief disclaimer. In this class, I won't be giving any tips about marriage. I hope this won't disappoint anyone, but it's partly because I don't have a perfect marriage myself. In fact, right now it's really struggling, and unfortunately there's no one-size-fits-all manual to fix it."

Millie sat up straight. She intuitively knew she had picked the right class. Nadine pulled out a Bible and stack of papers from her bag, placing them in front of her.

"But I do believe relationships, including marriage, can be

helped by having a close relationship with our Creator. He loves his creation and wants to relate to us. It's important to start *here*—not with the goal of saving our marriages or fixing other people, but to work on *ourselves* first. The desire for family, friendship—even romance—exists in us because it first exists in God. It's built into humans as much as it's built into his own being. It drives everything, and when people lose a connection with God—or allow that connection to be distorted by lies—it causes all kinds of dysfunction in the way people relate to each other."

Nadine took a deep breath, and Millie picked up her pen.

Something told her to play close attention.

"Like some of you, I'm guessing, I come from a broken family. And as long as I can remember, I never felt seen, you know—*really* seen or understood. Especially by my father, who I barely knew. I don't want to go into details, but in my desperation for love and attention, I did things I'm not proud of—things that hurt myself and others."

Nadine paused, a sadness passing across her eyes. She asked if anyone else in the room could relate to her story so far. More people than Millie expected raised their hands. She almost raised both of hers.

"Well, fortunately, my story doesn't end there," Nadine continued, her voice turning cheerful again. "When I was twenty-four, I cleaned house for two older sisters from Germany who knew what a train wreck I was but didn't judge me. They were the first people who ever explained to me—in a way that made sense—that God cared about me and wanted to have a relationship with me. They even highlighted a few specific times in my life when they thought God had been trying to get my attention. I was intrigued.

"So, one evening, I was reading a little New Testament they gave me. 'Focus on ze red letters,' one of the sisters had told me. 'Zey are ze vords of God's Son.' By sunrise, I had fallen in love. Jesus was more incredible than I'd ever imagined! Aside from offending religious leaders, I could hardly believe that someone so good and kind would suffer such a cruel, unjust death. Later, I learned that it was the extreme cost Jesus had to pay to define love, and hopefully win our hearts."

Nadine stood and, in her excitement, seemed to float around the room as she passed out papers. Millie glanced toward the door, wondering how far the bathroom was. Her bladder ached from the iced tea at lunch, but she didn't move. Nadine had the sincerity of an angel, the passion of her friend Bernie, and she looked like Stella.

Leaving felt harder than staying.

"I'm going to read some passages from the Bible," Nadine continued. "You can follow along on the handout if you wish. Each one speaks to how God can be related to, first as a loving and just father—the most common theme in the Bible—but also as a nurturing mother, a brother, or a friend. There are even passages where God is described as a faithful husband and lover! So, let's dive right in..."

Millie listened as best she could. As soon as the class ended, she bolted for the bathroom. By the time she found Frank, she was encouraged.

"I liked the class a lot," she told him, her voice upbeat. For the first time in a long time, she felt a spark of hope.

*God can be known, personally? He wants to be my father? I could be his daughter?*

These concepts hadn't lit a raging fire in her heart—not yet— but what Millie had heard that afternoon was a major jolt to her long-held agnostic beliefs about God.

~

THE LAST DAY of the conference arrived with cooler, more refreshing air. As often happens with retreats or camps, everyone felt like family, and they were reluctant to leave each other.

While Frank went to pick up the kids, Millie waited in the lounge area. Several people were sitting on a large sectional sofa, including Sarge and Marge, engaged in a lively conversation about God. Curious, Millie drifted closer. Marge spotted her and waved her over, patting the seat beside her.

At the center of the group sat a distinguished older man with a relaxed demeanor and a Bible in his lap. His white hair and beard contrasted handsomely with his youthful, casual attire, which included shorts and flip-flops.

He was speaking to a younger man who looked nervous in a suit and tie. A quiet, doe-eyed girl sat beside him.

"Danny," the older man said, "Jesus touches on what we're discussing in one of his parables. Do you have time for me to read it?"

Danny looked at his watch and nodded.

"Great," the man said, flipping through his Bible. "Okay, here it is. The book of Matthew, chapter 13. I'll paraphrase to keep it brief. Basically, Jesus tells us of a farmer who goes into a field to scatter seed—using a 'casting' method, as they did back then. Some seed falls on a footpath—never sprouts, of course, because it's either trampled or eaten by birds. Other seed falls on rocky soil—which sprouts quickly, but withers in the hot sun because the roots are too shallow. Still more seed falls among thorns, where the young plants get choked out."

He leaned in and gently touched Danny's knee to make sure he and his wife were listening.

"But Danny, Beth, listen to this," he said, tapping the page. "There's a fourth place where the farmer's seed fell: *good* soil, *fertile* soil. The plants that grew there matured and bore fruit. Do you see what I mean, friend? *That's* what we need: an honest, pure-hearted response to God and his words. Otherwise, we won't be changed. Truth will just go in one ear and out the other, quickly forgotten— like the seed on the path. Or we'll wither away when life get too hard—like the seed that landed on the rocky soil. Or—like the seed among thorns—our spiritual life will be choked by the love of money and other distractions, leaving us weak and unfruitful. Now do you understand?"

Danny looked at Beth, who gave a weak smile. Neither of them seemed particularly moved. Inside Millie, however, lightbulbs were turning on. She and Frank had planted their very first garden that year—a challenging yet rewarding project. They dug out rocks, fertilized the soil, pulled weeds, and even built a scarecrow to keep the birds away. By summer's end, their hard work had paid off in an abundance of preserved vegetables for the winter.

Until now, she'd never seen gardening as a spiritual metaphor.

The older man glanced at Millie, noticing the look on her face. He gave her a quick wink before turning back to the others. Millie rested her hand over her heart, which was burning. Everything she'd heard in the past five minutes—though not aimed at her—had pierced her heart like a fiery arrow. It ignited a single, all-consuming desire:

*She wanted good soil in her heart.* She wanted the truths God had shown her that weekend to take root and change her.

Millie stood and exchanged goodbyes with Marge, Sarge, Nadine, and a few others she had grown close to. Then she stepped outside to wait for Frank. The sweet fragrance of honeysuckle wafted from a nearby garden, which she inhaled deeply.

*What a surprising weekend,* she thought, her heart full of gratitude. She also felt a wave of relief that it was over. So much emotion... so much to think about.

*Please, God, let it not all be in vain!*

# CHAPTER 22

# A Divine Touch

S hortly after the conference, Millie stood at the front door watching Pamela and Frankie run down the gravel driveway which was lined on both sides with newly planted pine trees. Frankie grabbed a handful of grass and flung it at his sister. Pamela tried to trip him in return. Then they disappeared into the small school bus waiting at the end of the driveway.

It was mid-September, a time when the routine of most mornings was as ordinary as the rising sun. Frank would leave for work as dawn tinged the treetops in the back woods. Millie would wake in time to make sure he packed leftovers for his lunch. Then, once the kids were off to school, Millie would spend the rest of the morning on the countless tasks a good wife and mother does to prepare for her family's return.

However, this wasn't a typical morning. After the bus turned the corner, Millie returned to her bedroom. She didn't care about the messy kitchen. She didn't pull out dinner to thaw or start the laundry. None of her usual to-do's even crossed her mind. Only one thing pressed in on her: she'd been restless since the conference and she knew why.

*God was pursuing her.* And if her guess was correct, she had to stop running from him if she was to get any peace.

She sat on the edge of her unmade bed. The house was quiet and still except for the ticking of the grandfather clock dow the hall. Even the distant rumble of thunder and whispering breeze through the window made it feel like the whole world was holding its breath.

Millie reached for her pillow, still damp from tears shed in a sleepless night, and hugged it tightly.

"God," she cried out into the stillness, "I'm here. Please help me. I'm still feeling depressed. I really need something to change. Can you do something with my life? Is there hope for me?"

Frustration welled up. So many reasons to resist God marched in her head like a well-trained army. Thirty years of dysfunction had left wounds so deep, a fresh start felt like a fantasy.

*Or was it?*

Millie knew about God's love. In fact, she hoped in it, reading Nadine's handout at least a dozen times. It was just hard for her to see *her* life as worth saving. Not with *her* story and upbringing. Not with *her* failures and sins.

"Enough!" she burst out. "I'm sick of going in circles!"

The breeze outside shifted direction, sucking the curtains against the screen. She fell back onto the bed and stared at the ceiling, her eyes red and burning. As she rubbed them, something came to mind—something she'd once seen on a bookmark:

*"I am the good Shepherd, and my sheep hear my voice. I will call each of them by name, and I will lead them out."*

She had no argument for this. Even at her lowest, she'd always sensed someone there. It's what kept her going, what held despair at bay, and what kept hope alive. Jesus had even sent her wise "ewes"—

Aunt Ethel, Stella, Bernie, Nadine—to guide her and gently lead her back to him.

"Thank you, Jesus," Millie whispered, feeling humbled by this realization.

Mentioning his name triggered another memory—the backyard cross her cousins slapped together and their obscure, taunting words: "Bastard blood for bastard blood."

The handout from Nadine's class was still on her nightstand. Millie reached for it and found the verse where Jesus said:

*"Who are my brothers, my sisters, my mother? They are all those who do the will of my Father in heaven."*

Something clicked.

Even though Jesus had been raised by earthly parents, he never truly belonged to them. He was God's son, made human for a short time, and people accused him of being a bastard child—just like her!

But unlike her, Jesus didn't lash out when mistreated. Even as he died a criminal's death, he showed mercy.

*"Father, forgive them,"* he prayed through his battered, bloody face. *"They don't know what they're doing!"*

Millie lay flat on the bed as the realization descended on her like soft rain: if Jesus was God, then God wasn't angry with her. He loved her. He *really* loved her!

With fingers entwined around her pillow, Millie began to respond to this new revelation. She whispered the words, "I am *his*, I am *his*," until a switch flipped, and she was saying, "I am *yours*, I am *yours!*"

*And that's when it happened.*

In the years to come, Millie would often talk about this moment that changed her life forever. It was the moment the living Jesus came into her physical room, and into her physical body, delivering her from a lifetime of accumulated guilt, shame, anger, and unworthiness—all the "yuck," as she called it. Like a flood of liquid love, it surged into her mind, flowed through her body, and poured straight out her feet.

When it passed, it left her feeling washed and clean—like a newborn baby.

She lay still for a few minutes blinking in amazement. Then she stood, feeling light as a feather. The burden she'd been carrying for so long was *gone!*

She ran to the phone on the wall, lifted the receiver, and called Frank at work. *She had to tell someone!*

"Frank, something happened to me!" she gasped. "I don't know how to explain it, but Jesus washed me clean. I feel like a brand-new person!"

Frank didn't say much on the other end. He didn't know what to say.

Meanwhile, Millie hung up the phone, stood in the middle of the kitchen floor, *and danced*. At first, it was just a little movement in her upper body, like she was still afraid of upsetting an angry woman beneath an attic floor. But soon, the jiggles of joy moved to her socked feet and she was stomping and whirling with complete abandon!

# CHAPTER 23

# Migrant Work

T he morning air was crisp and cool. Millie stood in a field, wearing fingerless gloves and a red hat that matched her flushed cheeks and nose. Beneath her work boots, the dry soil crunched, thirsty for the softening rains of spring.

With stiff fingers, Millie reached into her waist pouch, pulled out a length of twine, and secured a dangling vine to a wire trellis. Then she took a few steps and repeated the task with another vine.

As she worked, she hummed her new favorite song:

*"As the deer panteth for the waters, so my soul longeth after you. You alone are my heart's desire, and I long to worship you."*

Working two rows over were José and his wife, Carlota, both from Mexico. They, along with a group of others in the field, were migrants. Every year they arrived on a bus from the south to help prune the vineyards and apple trees of upstate New York. At the bottom of a large hill, sheltered from brisk seasonal winds, they lived in a row of barracks provided by the landowner. Once they finished a job, they had to pack up and move to another farm that needed them.

These hardy, sun-weathered laborers didn't know what to make of the thirty-one-year-old white woman working alongside them. She was a clearly new at pruning and tying grapevines, but she showed up every weekday morning, whistling and eager to practice some more. She told them she was just trying to earn some "piggy bank money" while her kids were at school.

There was more to it, though. Time spent in the fresh air, among grapevines, under an open blue sky with honking geese passing over, stirred something in Millie's spirit. She felt it gave her a more nuanced understanding of Jesus' parables, especially the ones about pruning and bearing fruit.

José worked his way down the row until he stood across from her.

"¡Hola, Millie!" he called and waved, "What good news you have me today?"

He flashed a wide grin with a couple of missing teeth.

Millie smiled and waved back. Every day, in some small way, she'd been talking to José, Carlota, and their friends about Jesus. They were curious too; right from the start they wanted to know what songs she was singing and why she was so happy.

One Sunday stood out: she and Frank had brought a home-cooked ham dinner to the barracks, complete with all the sides. They even brought Pamela and Frankie. After everyone had their fill, the workers eagerly gathered around Millie to hear her story.

*Good news?* Millie thought, considering José's question. She'd been so used to focusing on bad news all her life, it was still hard to believe how much *good news* she had to share now!

While she bent over a particularly stubborn vine, José nicked his finger with his knife.

"Jesus Christ!" he cursed—something he often did, and always in surprisingly clear English. When he saw Millie stand up with concern, he quickly added, "I okay, no blood."

"Good," Millie said, then instinctively asked, "Do you know how much Jesus loves you, José?"

José chuckled. The funny white woman asked him that question every time he said "Jesus Christ." He already knew the answer.

"This much," he grinned, stretching out his arms as wide as they would go.

Millie laughed. "And that's because...?"

"I know. Because *God doesn't make junk,*" he said, finishing the line with her.

Millie watched him move down the row, smiling to himself as his calloused hands expertly trimmed the vines. Oh, how she loved this humble man, his wife, and all the migrant workers. She didn't care about their race or social standing, or even if they cursed or chewed tobacco. Ever since discovering how freely she was loved and forgiven—with no need to "measure up" to some religious standard —Millie wanted *everyone* to know they could be, too.

In a way, too, Jesus had also been a migrant. He traveled from place to place with no permanent home, a band of friends at his side. Millie could relate—not with the "band of friends" part yet— but to the feeling of being a stranger in a foreign land. Nobody she knew, not even Frank, shared her excitement about Jesus. It was like she spoke another language.

Frank, for his part, felt like a foreigner for a different reason. He struggled with his wife's dramatic change and her radical beliefs. He didn't feel like he fit into her life anymore. She wasn't the same woman with the same problems he'd always been her "savior" for.

And he wondered, did she even need him at all?

∽

"Do you know what I think?" Nellie asked after Millie mentioned Jesus for the third time that afternoon. She and Chuck were visiting one Saturday, sharing finger foods around the dining room table. She glanced over at a somber Frank. "I think Millie's been abducted by aliens!"

Millie giggled—just as freely as she would've years ago if someone had accused her of such a thing. Back in their teens, she and Nellie were obsessed with extraterrestrials, spending hours planning what they'd do if they were ever abducted. The scenario always played out the same: Millie would take charge and fight off the aliens while Nellie would go along with whatever plan Millie had made.

Frank forced a smile. To him, Nellie's suggestion wasn't completely off-base. In fact, it seemed more reasonable than believing his wife was having an affair—*with God!*

Later, when he and Chuck sat outside in lawn chairs cracking open cold beers, Frank let some of his frustration slip out. "All she talks about is Jesus," he said. "She says the Bible contains 'love letters' to her. I mean, what's a guy supposed to do with that?"

Frank immediately regretted his words, as Chuck ran with them.

"Man," he said, "I wouldn't tolerate living with a religious nut. My first girlfriend went bonkers like that when she stopped drinking. I put my foot down, yes siree...."

For the next few minutes Frank tuned Chuck out, which wasn't hard—the man could ramble nonstop. But mostly, it was because the story turned into a cold blow-by-blow of how he dumped his girlfriend because of her faith.

That wasn't what Frank wanted.

Sure, Millie could be intense about her beliefs. But something had clearly changed her. Something had pulled her out of a long depression and made her a more loving, grounded person.

So why couldn't he just be happy for her?

With some time to think, Frank realized the truth: he felt lost. He didn't have the kind of lively relationship with God that Millie had, and it rattled him. Being Catholic and living a decent life—these were the things he'd always leaned on. But Millie kept saying he needed to be "born again," whatever that meant. She tried to explain it meant letting go of his opinions, traditions, pride—*everything he was comfortable with*—to start a brand-new life as a student of Christ, following his ways.

It all sounded too radical at first. Frank was determined, instead, to live with Millie as peacefully as he could while hoping she'd return the favor.

Until a revolutionary thought surfaced. If God truly wanted a relationship with him, it wouldn't necessarily look like Millie's. It would be personal to *him.* And whatever change might come from giving his life to God—whether subtle or profound—would be up to God.

And that, Frank realized, he could accept.

So, with all this taking shape inside him, Frank had his own spiritual breakthrough several months later. It wasn't as dramatic as Millie's. Nor did he have a pile of crumpled tissues to show for it. But as he sat alone on a park bench in Rochester during his lunch break, his brief tears were enough. He *wanted* to know God. He *wanted* God to know him. And deep down, he also wanted to take his wife's hand—the one growing calloused from her mornings in the vineyard—and walk alongside her in a new relationship with God.

# CHAPTER 24

# Excommunication

A peculiar building loomed ahead, its tall, sharply pitched A-frame roof topped with a twisted metal cross. As soon as Pamela spotted it, she set aside her magnetic car bingo board.

"We're almost there," she told Frankie, opening her crocheted purse to pull out a rosary, a gift from her first communion. "I like this one. See the little Jesus and Mary charms on it?"

From the driver's seat, Frank chimed in. "Do you still carry the big ones in your back pockets?"

"No." Pamela giggled, "I'm wearing a dress."

She knew her dad was teasing her about the ten-inch plastic figurines of Jesus and Mary she used to dote on. She'd polish them, tuck them into bed each night, and once had even brought them to public school for fourth-grade show-and-tell.

"This is Jesus," she boldly told her classmates. "And this is Mary. And let me tell you *all* about who they are!"

After that, she was given the nickname: "Jesus freak."

"Hey, aren't we going to church?" Frankie asked, looking disappointed as they passed by the building. He and Pamela had enjoyed going ever since the children's school had moved to the basement. The priest, hoping to harness Millie and Frank's "spiritual zeal," had let them use the lower level to lead music for the kids: Frank on the guitar and Millie with the tambourine. They'd even started leading an adult Bible study focused on the "red letters" of Jesus.

Frank glanced in the rearview mirror. "We're trying somewhere new today, remember?"

The kids fell silent, then returned to their game. Little did they know what kind of rollercoaster ride lay ahead as their parents tried to figure out where they truly belonged.

"I still can't believe we got excommunicated," Millie said, breaking the silence. She had been quietly filing her nails. "I just couldn't bow down to that thing one more time. It felt so wrong."

Frank, focused on navigating a new route, nodded. He also was surprised when the priest called the week before to say they weren't welcome back. But it wasn't because he felt wronged. After all, walking out during Mass as the priest carried the monstrance down the aisle was hardly acceptable behavior. Plus, for months, he and Millie had naively believed that their fresh understanding of the Bible could somehow overturn two thousand years of church dogma.

In another time and place, they might've been burned at the stake!

No, what really surprised Frank was that he was no longer in the Catholic faith. It wasn't a future he had ever imagined for himself.

Millie examined her nails one last time. Frank noticed the pout on her face and couldn't resist teasing. He knew a reference to the priest's grim comment about her afterlife would get a rise out of her.

"Well," he said with a smirk, "at least I still have hope for heaven, seeing I was born Catholic. *If* I return to the church, of course."

Millie shot him a smoldering "you better be kidding" look and tossed her nail file into her purse.

"It's all just ridiculous, if you ask me," she said flatly.

"Yeah, ridiculous," he echoed, pulling sharply into a parking lot and snagging an open spot.

The new church, a plain three-story brick building, looked nothing like a Catholic church. And it was going to be different in other ways, too. Frank felt more nervous than he let on.

Frankie unbuckled his seatbelt.

"Wedicaliss, Wedicaliss," he repeated, amused by the sound of the word.

"Re-dic-ú-lous," Pamela corrected, exiting the car and slamming the door behind her. She stood waiting with a furrowed brow. The kids didn't fully grasp everything their parents talked about, but Pamela, being a little older, sensed that change was coming. And she, like her dad, usually expressed her feelings in quiet, indirect ways.

Millie pulled down the sun visor and quickly checked herself in the mirror.

"Even here we have to be careful of being spiritually deceived," she reminded Frank as he got out of the car. "There are many angels in sheep's clothing out there."

Frank came around the car and opened Millie's door. "Wolves," he corrected. "It's *wolves* in sheep's clothing."

Millie followed Frank, her head bowed against the wind. Normally, they both would have laughed at her verbal slip-up, but the morning felt strangely tense.

For weeks, Millie had been nagged by a feeling she couldn't quite name. It was as if something was quietly nipping at her spiritual life: tiny, painless bites that slowly eroded her joy and peace. Life had felt simpler when it was just her and God... exhilarating, even. She had a heavenly Father to discover and an adventure of learning to be his daughter. It was so easy back then to spend hours alone with her Bible, the world on pause, wrapped up in the wonder of a honeymoon with God.

*But lately...*

Climbing the steps, Millie's grip tightened around her purse strap. It wasn't that she'd lost her closeness with God. No one was dragging her to church either, any more than you could drag a wild horse. It was just that following Jesus had become more complicated. She wasn't a lone sheep on the path anymore. She was part of a flock—a "family," as Christians called it—and many of them were so different. Some even hard to love.

As she stepped through the doors of the new church, greeted by smiling ushers handing out bulletins, a tightness gripped her shoulders. She returned their smiles even as the weight of a thousand expectations settled on her like a suffocating blanket. Deep down, she knew things would get bumpy again.

"Family" was still a word she was learning to wrap her life around.

# CHAPTER 25

# Ride in a Police Car

A red-faced man in uniform stood at the front door, shifting awkwardly on his feet. Behind him, a patrol car idled in the driveway.

"Ma'am, is your name Mildred Anna Spock?"

Millie stepped back, her heart skipping a beat. The officer followed her inside and removed his hat.

"Yes, I'm Millie," she replied, her voice tight. "What's this about?"

"I'm sorry, ma'am, but I'm afraid I have to ask you to come with me."

Frank appeared at the top of the stairs and walked down to stand beside Millie. Pamela and Frankie, alarmed by the sight of a police officer at their home, hurried from their rooms and watched from the top of the landing.

The officer cleared his throat and explained that a check Millie had written to the small grocery store in town had bounced. The owner was pressing charges—for $7.85.

"You've got to be kidding me," Frank argued, his face flushing as red as the officer's. "We'll pay the bill right now."

The officer explained it was policy; Millie had to settle the debt in person at the sheriff's office before the charges could be dropped.

Millie grabbed her coat and purse, insisting Frank stay with the kids. As the patrol car backed out of the driveway, she looked up from the back seat and saw three anxious faces pressed against the big picture window waving goodbye.

A couple of hours later, the same officer dropped Millie back home. As soon as she stepped through the door, she marched straight to the phone book determined to confront the store owner.

Frank followed, his voice soft but cautious. "Listen, hon, do we really have to do this right now? It's too late in the day. Tomorrow I can go with you to—"

"Help me find the number, please. Now."

"Millie—"

"Stop. I'll be nice, I promise."

Sighing, Frank found the number. Millie dialed it, then rolled her eyes when she got the answering machine. She took a deep breath.

"Larry, this is Millie Spock. My number is 716-550-5289. Please call me back. It's important. Bye."

"Good," Frank said after she hung up. "You'll be calmer in the morning. We wouldn't want Rusty the Bailiff coming back to arrest you for harassment!"

Millie grunted and grabbed her apron. She'd been in the middle of cleaning out the cupboards when this ridiculous interruption happened. Now, with less than one hour before dinner, her project would have to wait.

Frank watched as she yanked out an absurdly long trail of paper towels from the roll.

"Hey," he asked carefully, "you're not rethinking the move to Colorado, are you? You're still good with it, right?"

Millie wiped her brow. "Yeah, I'm fine. It's just that there's so much to do! Can you believe it's almost May? We must get this place ready to rent in just four weeks. And I still want you to paint the foyer. I *hate* looking at those smudges!"

Frank walked off, shoving his own to-do list in his pocket.

He didn't see the need to paint the foyer. To him, a few scuff marks on a house barely seven years old were as harmless as freckles on a baby.

So why were they leaving it all to go to Colorado?

It had seemed like a crazy idea at first, sparked one Sunday when the pastor announced that their church had launched a new satellite location in Denver, which needed help. While it wasn't China—a country Frank had long dreamed of going to as a missionary—Colorado made sense. He could see how the "wild west" might be his training ground.

And pioneer that Millie was, she caught the bug too. Discontent had been brewing in her over the church they'd been attending since leaving Catholicism. It was big, and they didn't feel needed. The church in Denver was small, and it needed help. Maybe in this new place they could *finally* use their gifts to serve God and his people?

Frank headed downstairs to gather his painting supplies. There was just enough time in the day to paint the foyer.

THE NEXT MORNING arrived with an ambush, literally: a late-April squall that came out of nowhere. Millie slept in, but Frank, on his way to work, was blinded by the snow and had to pull over. The storm also delayed the kids' school bus.

Destiny wasn't on winter's side, however. Spring was the victor. By the time Millie woke up, the storm had fled, and a triumphant sun was already melting the snow into slushy submission.

The kids had meanwhile thrown together their own lunches

and were waiting at the door for the bus. Millie came out in her bathrobe and slippers, poured herself a cup of coffee, and sat with them. Frankie chattered on about the storm his mom had missed, sipping milk through a straw in his favorite 7-Eleven "Big Gulp" cup. At thirteen, it seemed like he was going through a cow a day. Pamela, nearing the end of ninth grade, was silent, staring glumly out the window. She wasn't happy about her parents' decision to move to Colorado. Millie noticed her shirt was unbuttoned by three holes and her collar was flipped up again: both "preppy" trends which Pamela snuck in when her father wasn't around.

"It's coming," Frankie said, the first to notice the spot of yellow turning onto Smith Hill Road. He and Pamela hurried out to meet it.

Millie got up and carried her empty mug back to the kitchen. As she passed the foyer, she caught a whiff of fresh paint. *Ah, the smell of gratitude!* Frank might have found the task trivial, but removing those small smudges made Millie's burden feel lighter. She even felt like she could put aside her list for a few minutes and start her day with God and his words.

After pouring another cup of coffee, she slid a stool out from under the breakfast bar and sat down. In front of her was her large-print, leather-bound, *Thompson Chain-Reference King James Version Study Bible...* made even bulkier by all the pens and notes tucked between its pages. Frank liked to tease her about its size, saying things like, "It's larger than a breadbox," or "if you drop it on someone's foot, it'll break it!" But Millie wasn't deterred. She hauled her behemoth Bible wherever she thought she needed it... which, frankly, was everywhere.

As her fingers flipped through the large, well-worn pages, Millie thought about "little Larry," the short-statured man whom she expected to call back any minute. Frank was partly right; she did feel calmer that morning, even a little amused. A stay-at-home mom being hauled away in a police car over $7.85? It was so absurd, she wondered if Pamela and Frankie might tell the story to their own kids someday!

The other part of Millie wasn't amused. What Larry had done was wrong—even cruel. Her phone number was on the check. They had a working answering machine. So why hadn't he called before going to the police?

*He doesn't like me,* Millie thought, flipping through the pages. Her brow furrowed. *He just wanted to be mean and spiteful to show it!*

She abruptly stopped, then pulled out a highlighter.

"Ah, there it is," she muttered, tapping the page. It was time to wave the surrender flag.

Despite her assumptions about Larry, Millie had woken that morning with the conviction to handle the situation with some dignity. And the Bible verse she had just found confirmed this.

She slowly read the words as she streaked them with yellow:

*"You have heard it once said, 'Love your friends but hate your enemy.' But I say to you, love your enemies, bless those who curse you, do good to those who hate you, and pray for those who spitefully use you and persecute you, so that you may become sons of your Father in heaven. For He makes His sun to rise on the evil and on the good, and sends rain on the just and the unjust."*

Loving enemies wasn't always easy for Millie. She'd experienced miraculous success with people like the uncle who had abused her—a forgiveness that came almost instantly after she first encountered Christ. But "little Larrys" and arrogant, back-biting church women? For some reason they were more challenging.

Still, she knew if she focused on Jesus and how much he loved *her*, she could love anyone. Even just reading Jesus' words that morning, she felt her heart soften toward Larry. By the time she rose to start the day, her heart felt lighter and the tension had melted from her face.

She walked to the counter, cut a thick slice of zucchini bread, and spread soft butter over the top. All around the kitchen was clutter that hadn't passed her "one-wagon gypsy test" from the day before. Unless she wanted to serve her family TV dinners for a third night in a row, everything needed to be packed into long-term storage boxes as efficiently as possible.

She finished her breakfast and got to work.

A few hours later, the phone rang. Millie reached for the handset and with a deep breath reminded herself that if she were to give Larry any advice, it would be *loving* advice.

"Hello?" she answered.

"Hello, honey! It's me!"

Millie stiffened. "Mom?"

"Yes! I'm calling from my phone in Florida! I don't know why the harebrained operator couldn't find your number at first. I told her she must be blind not to see it and then *presto!* She found it. Can you believe it?"

Millie pulled out the counter stool—the same one she had spiritually steadied herself on that morning—and perched on its edge.

Toots babbled on, oblivious to Millie's stunned silence.

"I have good news," she said. "I got married! I did it last month at the Justice of the Peace here in Florida."

Millie slowly rubbed her forehead. Aside from exchanging Christmas and birthday cards, she hadn't meaningfully communicated with her mother in... how many years? Seven?

"Gerald Creamer is his name, or Jerry for short," Toots continued. "He's a retired postal worker who's never been married until now. We're driving up north for Memorial Day weekend to do some sightseeing. Jerry used to live in the Big Apple but has never been upstate. You live in Walworth, right? Let me see, I've got one of your cards here. Okay, yes, Walworth. Well, anyway, Jerry will handle the details. He says Sunday would be the best day. Right, Jerry? *Yes, I'm talking to Millie!* Oh, for God's sake, I already told you the TV wasn't working, remember? We need to get a new one..."

Millie chewed her bottom lip. Apparently, "conversation" with Toots was going to be the same as always. At the first lull, she jumped in.

"Actually, Mom, we're leaving for Colorado in early June, so things are hectic right now. It might be hard to do..."

Her voice trailed off. Would it really be that hard to throw together *one* dinner? They were coming a long ways, and besides— she hadn't told Toots about her experience with Jesus yet.

"...but maybe we can work something out," Millie finished, rising from the stool. "I'll check with Frank first, but dinner here should work. Yes? Okay, good. I have to go now, Mom. Call me when you arrive at your hotel in Rochester."

Millie hung up the phone and immediately dialed Frank. He could hear the nervous excitement in her voice as she replayed the events of the morning: from her attitude adjustment toward Larry to the surprise call from Toots. Frank did his best to focus while being distracted at work.

"Listen," he said, "whatever you decide is fine. It's terrible timing as you said, but if you're at peace about it I'll support it."

Millie hung up and slowly exhaled. *Was* she at peace about it? Honestly, she wasn't sure.

But expecting Larry and getting Toots didn't feel like an accident, either.

# CHAPTER 26

# Mildred Sr

Houses shouldn't float, but this one did. It hovered in the sky like a disembodied head, staring blankly through dark, hollow windows. When the wind passed through its rickety boards, a faint, mournful howl followed, and the loose shutters banged with a maddening rhythm.

It was a wretched scene. And even though it was only a dream, Millie didn't want to look at the house, let alone go inside it.

When she was a little girl, a print of a similar house had hung in their dining room. Taped to the frame was a poem Toots had clipped from a magazine. "The House with Nobody in It" by Joyce Kilmer was a melancholy piece which Toots liked to recite— especially to impress guests.

Millie couldn't help but remember parts of it; the words seemed to describe her bad days growing up:

*I never have seen a haunted house, but I hear there are such things;*
*That they hold the talk of spirits, their mirth and sorrowings.*
*I know this house isn't haunted, and I wish it were, I do;*

*For it wouldn't be so lonely if it had a ghost or two.*

This dream, beginning with the floating house, came just days after Toots's unexpected phone call. Although Millie would interpret it as a sign she was meant to see her mother again, it didn't make the dream less disturbing. The house in her dream, much like the one described in the rest of Kilmer's poem, was "weary and tired." Both had "shingles broken and black" choked by "vines needing to be trimmed and tied." Yet, there was something more sinister about the house in her dream.

*It wasn't empty.*

Through a window at the top, Millie saw children inside—dozens of them—crawling, squirming, and tumbling over each other like a writhing mass of earthworms.

She was trying to make sense of it when, suddenly, Toots appeared at the window. She was a teenager, her face streaked with mud and tears, holding something unformed and bloody in her hands.

Millie didn't know much about her mother's childhood. Aunt Mabel once told her that Toots had been a troubled, angry girl. After years of outbursts and misbehavior, her exasperated mother—divorced and overwhelmed—had sent her away to a state-run reformatory school in the Catskills. It was there, her aunt hinted, that something terrible happened; something that had caused Toots's fragile mental state to snap.

As soon as Millie saw Toots in the window, the dream shifted—or perhaps it was a new dream. Millie was standing, unseen, inside a cramped restroom. It looked like the back of a family-run upholstery business, with fabric rolls and sewing machines stacked in the hallway. A little girl around seven—*Toots again*—hurried in. She fumbled to lock the door but couldn't quite reach it.

Then a man pushed his way in. He closed the door, locked it, and greeted her by name.

Toots ran into the stall, trembling.

What happened next Millie saw from two angles, as dreamers easily do. She saw the man: leering, moving slow, savoring the chase. And she saw Toots: quaking behind the curtain, fear contorting her face. It wasn't a fear of the unknown, however. It was an experienced fear; the kind that flinched with every counted footstep and knew to wipe the tears from her face before the curtain was pulled back.

The split second before she did so, Toots's countenance changed. Her facial expression hardened. She squared her shoulders, clenched her fists, and raised her chin in defiance. What started off as the look of a helpless child, was quickly replaced by a cornered dog snarling through pain and rage.

At this horrific moment Millie woke up.

"Oh my God. She's broken!" she gasped, sitting upright.

Frank jolted awake.

"Wha—what is it?" he stuttered. "What's wrong?"

Millie gushed out the dream, breathless, then finished by saying again, *"She's broken! So, so broken!"*

Why she kept repeating this, she didn't know, but it was years later that she would realize something extraordinary. Her subconscious mind must've been echoing the final line of Kilmer's poem!

*I never go by the empty house without stopping and looking
    back,*
*Yet it hurts me to look at the crumbling roof and the shutters
    fallen apart,*
*For I can't help thinking the poor old house is a house with a
    broken heart.*

Millie left Frank to sob in the living room. She cried not only for Toots, but for herself and every child who'd ever suffered sexual abuse. This wasn't the first time she had done this—Millie had an especially sensitive heart over this issue. She'd been known to pray all night for a kidnapped child on the news.

But seeing Toots as a victim? *That* was new. She never imagined her as a "poor old house with a broken heart." It was an image that fundamentally changed Millie's heart toward the woman who raised her.

When Toots and Jerry visited a week later, a more empathetic Millie opened the door. She served beef stew, cheesy bread, and a store-bought apple pie with vanilla ice cream. Pamela and Frankie reconnected with their grandmother. And they all met her new husband, too: a serious man who didn't seem eager to embrace a new family.

Despite the awkwardness, they all said their goodbyes with promises to stay in touch.

"That wasn't so bad," Frank said, helping Millie clean up afterward. He grabbed dishes from the table. "Your mother seemed on good behavior for once. She watched her mouth, at least."

Millie, hands in sudsy water, nodded. "Yeah, but did you notice how weak she's gotten? There's no way she'll jump on car hoods anymore. And Jerry, he's kind of a miserable coot, isn't he? I doubt she'll be beating *him* up."

Frank set a tray of dishes beside her, then wrapped his arms around her waist. "I'm glad you're not jumping on car hoods anymore yourself. Or beating me up. I'm proud of you."

Millie smirked as he walked off to grab a towel.

"Do you think your mother will ever fess up about your birth?" he asked when he came back.

"I don't know," she said, handing him a plate. "She's still proud. But who knows? Miracles happen. One did with me."

Frankie wandered in for a drink of water.

"It was weird seeing Grandma," he said casually. "I barely remember her."

He took a sip, then added, "Funny how they're moving here when we're leaving."

Frank turned around. "Moving here? What are you talking about?"

Frankie's eyes widened. "Uh... she told us that. In the living room. She sat between me and Pam and slipped us each twenty bucks. Said, '*When I move back to New York, I'll have more where this came from.*'"

"I didn't hear anything about her moving here," Millie said, frowning.

Frank shrugged. "Well, I don't think we have anything to worry about. Colorado is a long, safe distance from New York!"

# CHAPTER 27

# Rocky, Rocky Mountains

Frank hoisted a bag of tools into the back of his pickup and strapped an aluminum ladder onto the rack. He stepped into the garage for his water jug.

"Is your mother up yet?" he asked Millie.

Sweat glistened on Frank's forehead. It was only 8 a.m. but already the Colorado sun was making their housing development feel like an afternoon desert.

Millie was in the garage scooping bird pellets into a bucket. For a perfectly natural reason, her hobby of owning white doves—"love birds" as they were aptly called—had hatched into a small business. The two monogamous birds bred so often that she had to sell their chicks to a pet store. Frank thought they were a waste of time; although truth be told, he just hated the male's relentless, noisy mating ritual.

For Millie, the extra cash was worth the inconvenience. It was a tough season, and it didn't help that their church was in the middle of *another* series on tithing.

She grimaced as she struggled to pry open a bid lid. "She's watching the news with her tea. Jerry's still sleeping."

"I forgot—what time is their flight again?"

"Three o'clock on Saturday, right after Pamela's graduation. Not much longer now."

"Counting the minutes."

"You'll be done with your painting job by noon, right? They want to see downtown Denver. Then we can go to Casa Bonita for an early dinner. It'll be cheaper then."

Frank nodded. "Easily by noon. But I need to be back around six to make it to the elder's meeting on time. And don't forget, we also have the youth group coming over at seven. Your mom and Jerry can watch their TV shows then."

Millie carelessly bumped into her bucket, spilling seed across the floor. She groaned, a tightness rising in her chest. *Will the pressure ever end?*

Two and a half years ago, they had leisurely driven to Denver like Jesus-loving hippies on an adventure, convinced they were doing something "important" for God. They had even made the trip in an orange Volkswagen camper van, the kind that hippies drove.

But almost immediately their lives became as frantic as a hamster on a wheel. Frank joined the church worship team within two months, was made an elder within six, and not long after that both he and Millie were leading the youth group.

They were well past burnout.

"We could cancel the youth meeting," Millie said gruffly.

Frank was gruff back.

"It's not a big deal. They'll just hang out in the basement. And I'll be back by seven-thirty."

*You're unsubmitted to your husband.*

Millie hadn't heard Frank say this; it was just an accusation that hovered in the air around her. Lately she'd been more vocal about problems at church, and not everybody appreciated her boldness.

Snatching the broom, she swept up the spilled seed.

*I should never have shared anything with Lilian,* she thought to herself, fuming. *Some friend she is, blabbing my concerns to her husband!*

Lilian was the wife of an elder—the elder who had "lovingly" informed Frank that he thought Millie had a "submission problem." When Frank later relayed this to Millie, she skipped both services that following Sunday—to Frank's embarrassment—as well as the midweek prayer meeting.

It hadn't been difficult for Millie to do. Whenever she smelled spiritual pride or manipulation her antennae went up, and if no one listened to her concerns, her wings would follow.

But the accusation still stung. She *wanted* friends. She *wanted* to belong. She just didn't want to turn a blind eye to dangerous issues. Didn't God want people to be honest? If they smelled smoke, shouldn't they call "fire"?

Frank saw the strain in her face. He felt bad for her. She was carrying an extra load of stress with her mother visiting.

*He too* was under pressure, though. Being in church leadership was tricky. With one ear he heard, "keep your wife in line," but with the other, he trusted Millie's discernment. He couldn't just dismiss her. Sure, she lacked the diplomacy and tact of other ministry wives, but she *was* a sharp woman. Trying to rein her in wasn't working; neither with the kids who were pushing for more freedom. Every effort to be a "godly" husband and father backfired. He was losing his family—*and for what?* A pat on the back from the pastor? From God? *Did God even expect all this?*

When Millie finished sweeping, Frank took the broom and hung it back on the wall.

"Listen," he said, "we have to just get through this weekend, okay? Next week is a slow one for me. After your mother leaves on Sunday, let's take the kids camping at Red Rocks."

Then he turned and left quickly, which was probably for the best. His past attempts to explain to Millie why he couldn't get enough painting jobs in Denver's booming suburbs never ended well. Besides, while he knew it was because big companies were low-balling and winning his bids, he too was frustrated by the irony of it.

Millie returned to the kitchen to find Toots opening and closing cupboards.

"Hungry, Mom?" she asked, setting her bucket near the door-way. "Want eggs? Or oatmeal?"

"Eggs over easy. Where's your sugar? This bowl's low, and hard at the bottom. You should put a marshmallow in it, you know."

Millie refilled the sugar bowl and started breakfast. Meanwhile, the conversation went as well as could be expected. At one point, there was even a rare chance to go deeper with Toots—a good one, too—but Millie was too spiritually drained to take it. Plus, why would this time be any different? The few times she'd tried to tell Toots what had happened to her, the response was always the same: "That's nice, dear," she'd say, followed by a quick change of subject that always seemed to include digging out her church membership card or reciting the Lord's Prayer.

A rooster crowed outside. Toots stretched her neck to peer through the second-story kitchen window.

Its view couldn't have been more different than the Spocks' home in New York. The tiny lawn was a treeless patch of dry grass bordered on all three sides by neighbors and a tall wooden fence. The only remarkable feature of this totally urban landscape was the sight of three chickens pecking around for bugs.

Toots didn't notice any of it. She turned back to the table. "We bought a double-wide in New York, you know."

"Yes, I know," Millie said wearily. She'd known about the move for over a year.

She set a platter with eggs, toast, and peach jam on the table.

"Help yourself, Mom. Here's the spatula. How do you pronounce the name of your town again? I always get it wrong."

"Honey-oye. It's in the Finger Lakes, near Bristol. Jerry wanted something in the country with a three-car garage for his books. He's an oddball; did you know he collects books?"

Millie bit her lip. Toots's memory seemed to be getting worse.

A figure appeared in the doorway.

"Speak of the devil!" Toots cackled when she saw Jerry. He was only half-wrapped in Frank's bathrobe, his hair disheveled. He mumbled something about wanting coffee. Millie got up to pour him a cup.

"What's with the rooster outside?" he grumbled. "I didn't order a wake-up call."

Millie teased that the rooster only crowed for "late birds," but Jerry's frown didn't budge. Despite his soft, padded appearance, he wasn't exactly a teddy bear—and he still refused to be called "Grandpa" or "Dad." Just Jerry.

As he shuffled off, Millie updated Toots on the day's plans.

"Once Frank gets home, we'll take a little tour of Denver. Then we'll have an early dinner at that Mexican place, the one in a castle with the shows. We just need to be back by six. Then at seven, some kids are coming over for a meeting in our basement."

"Kids?" Toots asked. "What do they do in your basement?"

Millie was surprised by Toots's question... more specifically, that she had asked a conversational-type question at all.

"Well, different things," Millie said cautiously, placing an egg on her plate. "They talk about God, sing, pray for each other. They even visit a nursing home twice a month."

She paused, feeling a flicker of pride. She really did like the young people. They were authentic, full of simple zeal for God and life... just like she had been as a new believer. If only they could stay that way, never becoming hypocrites or lifeless zombies like so many adults!

"You'd like them, Mom. They're good kids—really on fire for God."

Toots's eyes suddenly glazed over. Her expression went eerily distant. Then her lips curled back.

"*Fire!*" she hissed, dragging the word through clenched teeth.

Millie blinked, confused. "Uh... yeah, you know. Fire—passion? They're not perfect, but—"

Before she could finish, Toots grabbed her cane and raised it above her head. Her face twisted.

"Christians," she seethed, "are made to *stomp* on!"

Millie dropped her fork with a clatter. She couldn't believe what she had just heard. It wasn't her mother's voice! Thinking fast, she reached for the tools in her mental toolbox. This was a moment to address something she perceived was *not* her mother.

"Demon," Millie said firmly, "you listen up. Don't raise your voice in this house again. *Jesus Christ* is Lord here!"

For a moment, the room went still. Then, as quickly as Toots's features had contorted, they softened. She lowered her cane and, in her sweetest voice, said, "Well, honey, I'm feeling a little tired. I think I'll lie down for a bit before our road trip."

And just like that, she got up and hobbled out of the kitchen.

Pamela was sprawled on the couch around the corner, a calendar on her lap and papers piled everywhere. She was reviewing her graduation itinerary, planning a summer mission trip to Mexico, *and* drafting out the youth group's monthly newsletter. Her schedule was as packed as her parents'.

But what she heard from the kitchen was too concerning to ignore. When she had the chance, she went in. Her mom looked shaken, one hand covering her mouth.

"What was that about?" Pamela asked. "Why did you yell at Grandma?"

"I didn't yell. Did she say anything to you when she walked by?"

"No, nothing. She just gave me a little poke with her cane, and a wink. Why? What happened?"

In a hushed but excited voice, Millie told her everything. Pamela shook her head. She'd heard stories about her mom's past—including ones involving Toots—but this was an especially bizarre one.

"Has she ever talked in a different voice before?"

Millie tilted her head, trying to remember. "Not that I recall. Not like that. It was so strange, Pam—she didn't even hear my response!"

Toots fortunately had no more outbursts during her stay in Denver. In fact, she was as sweet as an angel, blessing Pamela and the whole family with generous gifts of cash.

The kitchen episode was never mentioned again.

Still, Millie couldn't shake what had happened. Growing up, she'd always sensed something was off about her mother—something deeper than a personality quirk. When "Borderline Personality Disorder" became a recognized psychiatric diagnosis in the early eighties, Millie was struck by how closely it fit Toots's volatile, manipulative behaviors, especially given its link to childhood trauma.

Even so, Millie felt the explanation went beyond a clinical label. It was also a spiritual matter to her... one that required a spiritual breakthrough. But how could she help her mother, or anyone else, when she felt so drained? Lately, she hadn't felt like the "warrior princess" a friend once called her, ready to "storm the gates of hell" for someone's deliverance. She was instead buried in distractions, tangled in church obligations, and increasingly unsure what side of the gate she was even on!

Something had to change. *But what? How?*

By the time her mother and Jerry were on their flight back to New York, Millie had made at least one hard decision.

And she knew Frank was *not* going to like it.

"SO, VALERIE CALLED YOU A WARRIOR PRINCESS?" Frank repeated, lifting a metal canteen to his lips for a quick sip. "That was nice of her, I suppose. I thought you two didn't get along?"

With their legs dangling over a cliff, Millie and Frank sat next to each other gazing out at a baby-blue, cloud-speckled sky. Beneath the clouds, the majestic Rocky Mountains stretched endlessly from north to south.

*Red Rocks Campground* had always felt like the Spocks' little secret—and a bit of a mystery, too. They never did figure out what had possessed them to drive up the dangerously steep, washed-out road to discover it. The undercarriage of their camper van had gotten damaged, there were no hookups for electricity or water at the top, and the bathroom? That was outside, under the stars, shared by the coyotes whose howls echoed through the campground every night.

Even so, the breathtaking view kept them coming back... along with their recurring need for spiritual refreshment.

"You're missing my point," Millie said, frustrated. "I don't know what it means to be a warrior, *or* a princess. The only fighting I'm doing lately is with you. And it's not pretty."

Frank wanted to lighten the mood. They'd been suffocating each other for far too long. He picked up a small stone and threw it off the ledge.

"What about the other day, with your mother?" he asked. "That took courage."

Millie wiped sweat from her brow.

"Maybe. I just wonder why it happened at all, you know? I feel like the enemy got a pigeonhole."

"Pigeonhole?"

She didn't answer.

"Okay," Frank went on. "So, what's this big thing you wanted to tell me?"

*It was time.* Millie took a deep breath, inhaling the clean scent of juniper and spruce. Off to the right of their lookout, Frankie and Pamela were climbing on a mass of smooth sedimentary formations that were beautiful, but especially dangerous at the higher elevations.

"Be careful, you two!" she shouted, "Don't go any higher without us!"

Another breath.

"I can't do it anymore, Frank. I just can't keep going to church like everything's fine. I need a break to clear my head and get strong. You can keep going; I'm not stopping you. But right now, my relationship with Christ is more important than being a Christian."

She swallowed, almost tasting the profoundness of this totally unplanned statement. Wearing the label "Christian" didn't make someone a true follower of Christ. It was like Keith Green once said:

*"Going to church doesn't make somebody a Christian, any more than going to McDonald's makes someone a hamburger."*

More than anything, Millie wanted to be the real deal. She wanted to embody the true meaning of the word "Christian" without its religious baggage. And she wanted to "do church" like Jesus did, too, whatever that meant.

The only way she knew how to sort everything out was to simply get off the religious merry-go-round… even if it meant others would see her as an apostate.

Frank pursed his lips, taking this announcement in. He fixed his eyes on the tallest mountain in view, the one with the heaven-dipped peak and frosty jags. Millie's words didn't shock him. She had already skipped several church events and social activities. But continuing in ministry without her? How could he explain *that?*

He glanced over at the kids, laying down on a rock looking bored. Then he turned back.

"Should we tell them now or later?"

Millie's eyes narrowed. "What are you talking about?"

"You know. Tell the kids we're moving back to New York?"

"What? Really? How...?"

Her heart skipped a beat. She hadn't expected him to say that.

"We've always talked about going back," Frank explained. "It feels like the right time. You're not happy here. Pamela just graduated and aside from her mission trip next month, she has no plans."

"And our lease ends in August!" Millie chimed in.

Frank sighed, tossing another pebble off the cliff.

"I just can't imagine going to church without you, Millie. We're a team. And you're right—my relationship with God isn't what it used to be either. I think I've been confusing pleasing the church with pleasing God. Maybe he'd rather we walk together in peace?"

Millie tingled with happiness. A string of silver-edged clouds drifted in front of the sun, casting swift, dappled shadows across the valley.

Frank stood up and held out his hand. "The kids are waiting. Before it gets dark, let's go to the next level with them."

She took Frank's hand.

*The next level?* That sounded like a heavenly adventure she was ready for!

# CHAPTER 28

# *Growing Pains*

Millie stood at the closed door of Pamela's room. It was quiet. Should she go in again? What would she say?

The poor girl had been holed up in there for days after a recent church event, crying and barely coming out to eat. Neither she nor Frank had been able to console her. If this pain was a part of their twenty-two-year-old daughter's spiritual growth, it was no less painful for them to watch.

Millie felt partly responsible. Soon after leaving Denver and returning to their home in Walworth, N.Y., they had grown restless again. Frankie was adjusting to his old school as a junior but had become more withdrawn. Pamela was frustrated over her lack of post-graduation dreams and plans. And Frank, having gone back to work, was drifting... like a shipman who diligently mopped the deck and maintained the rigging but had no idea where to steer the vessel.

All of this led them to ask the same questions all over again:

*How can a person be a faithful, genuine Christian and not regularly attend a church? Wasn't that the way people "worshipped" and served God? Wasn't attending meetings necessary to have meaningful fellowship with spiritual family?*

It was uncomfortable waiting for an answer, so they began attending a small church nearby. Unlike their time in Denver, however, they didn't get involved right away. A safe move? Not exactly.

Millie's struggle had always been what happened when a concern pressed against her burning heart. Whether she chose to sit in the front row or the back, it didn't matter. The fire inside her would spark her tongue, and she would eventually find herself in the hot seat again.

But *Pamela* in the hot seat—in the middle of a special church event? That had been excruciating to watch. A sword went through her own heart seeing her daughter get wounded in battle.

*Maybe I should've stopped her from going,* Millie thought. She and Frank were already disillusioned with the practice of elevating people in church... people eager to flash titles like "pastor," "prophet," or "minister of the gospel." They just never expected their daughter to have to learn this lesson the hard way.

Still lingering outside the door, Millie couldn't help but feel angry at how things had played out. She wished she could've shielded her daughter from feeling humiliated and manipulated.

"Knock knock," Millie said softly, cracking the door open. "You hungry? I made some turkey soup."

Pamela was sitting up in bed, books and papers scattered around her. She'd always been a reflective soul who needed a lot of time to journal, draw, and process in quiet.

"Come in, Mom," she said. Her eyes were wide and dry. She looked better than she had in days. "I've got something encouraging to share with you."

Millie sat on the edge of the bed and waited.

Pamela finished sorting her papers, then looked up, her voice steady and upbeat.

"So, Mom, it's taken me some time to work through everything, but I think I've turned a corner. The details don't matter anymore. It doesn't matter if a wrong was done. I learned a lesson, and I'm stronger for it. I learned how important it is to listen to God's voice for myself, and not just assume other people speak for God. Not even you and Dad."

Millie blinked rapidly. Hope stirred in her chest.

Pamela held up the papers, filled with scribbled references.

"All day I've been flipping through the Bible, front to back, looking for every verse that speaks about God's Spirit living inside us. Look at all of them! Isn't it cool? So many churches have it backwards, saying we enter the 'house of God' when we gather in a building. But that's not what Jesus taught. He said, 'The time is coming—and now is—when true worshippers *won't worship my Father in a place*, but they will worship him in *spirit* and in *truth*.' He didn't emphasize buildings, because *we* are his home!"

She was growing animated now, bouncing a little on the bed.

"Anyway, it's like you once said, Mom. My relationship with God is more important than 'being a Christian.' I must be true to God, and myself—even if that means being misunderstood or rejected by other people."

She paused, catching her breath. "I don't have all the answers. I don't know where I'll be in my understanding tomorrow or ten years from now. But I believe God will lead me and teach me what I need to know. And if I get off track, he's perfectly capable of bringing me back. I want him too!"

Millie raised a hand to her lips. She didn't want to breathe. Was she witnessing a miracle?

Pamela, along with Frankie, were both easygoing, non-confrontational kids. From early on, they'd been pressed, prodded (even guilted at times) into following rules and religious expectations... expectations that Millie and Frank were questioning or had already abandoned. Their stumbling, imperfect journey to be "good

Christians" and "good parents"—while still trying to grow up themselves—couldn't have been easy for their kids to go through. Millie often worried how their mistakes might have affected them.

She swallowed hard, blinking back tears.

"Are you okay?" Pamela asked.

"I'm fine, I mean, I'm good. It's just that..."

"What?" Pamela urged.

Millie steadied herself and smiled.

"I've just been worried, is all. That's what moms do. But seeing you like this—strong, bold, noticing many of the same things I've been seeing? I can't really explain it. I just feel happy."

What Millie struggled to express in that moment was a feeling that she didn't have words for yet; not until she had travelled further down the road and looked back. Then, she would have the words, and so would Pamela. They would both end up agreeing that a mother and daughter didn't just grow closer that day. They also stepped through a door to become friends and fellow-travelers together on the same spiritual journey.

# CHAPTER 29

# Amazing Grace

Dressed in polyester slacks, a sparkly sweater, and a matching scarf, Millie gently rocked on the porch swing. A large purse rested beside her, and from the eave, a windchime shaped like a camping trailer tinkled softly in the breeze.

She looked up at it. The words painted on the chime stirred her thoughts: *"Not All Who Wander Are Lost."*

Five years ago, Pamela's experience at their old church had triggered a profound shift in their spiritual journey. Soon after, Millie and Frank sold everything—including their house in Walworth—and embarked on a new adventure: traveling the country in a motorhome.

It had been a journey of learning and discovery. With Frankie in community college, Pamela joined them on the road. They crisscrossed the country, participated in craft shows, met fascinating people, and—perhaps most importantly—gained a deeper understanding of what "church" truly meant.

Nomadic life had its challenges, though. After about eighteen months, they decided to settle down again—this time in the Bristol Mountains of upstate New York.

It marked the beginning of a calmer, more grounded chapter.

As Millie reflected on all this, she attempted to whistle.

"Hey, Dilly-Dolly! Whatcha want, pretty girl?"

A hundred feet ahead, a mare whinnied behind a pasture gate, and beyond the pasture loomed a steep wall of trees mottled with early autumn color. Stretching the length of this vista was a state road lined on each side with goldenrods and purple asters.

Bristol Ski Mountain was just two miles down this road.

Millie squinted and spotted a few lifts moving slowly up and down the hillside. It was smart, she thought, to run them in the off-season for "leaf-peepers."

Plus, it brought much-needed tourism to their little store.

Getting up from the swing, Millie walked down the porch steps to a nearby hedgerow and picked a few wild apples for Dolly.

If she had a dollar for every time she pinched herself over owning a horse, she'd be black and blue—and she'd get her money back, too, since her sweet brown beauty had cost her only $300. Named after her childhood stick horse, Dolly was an ex-harness trotter with a limp. When a local racetrack retired a few horses, Millie jumped at the chance... and then jumped on Dolly! At forty-seven, Millie's dream of riding her own horse had finally come true —with enough land to enjoy it, too.

She returned to the swing just in time to see Frank coming up the walkway.

"What a view, huh?" he said. "It never gets old."

He wiped his brow, now a little grayer from caring for twenty-four acres and stocking their gift shop with his woodworking crafts. He loved it, though. His face had the look of a boy enjoying summers in the hills of Pennsylvania. It was as much a surprise to him as to anyone that they settled down again—and in such a beautiful place. China, Denver... those missionary dreams were behind him now. He was content to stay right where he was for the rest of his life.

"Ready to see your mother?" Frank asked. "I put the closed sign on the store."

"Yes," Millie said, rubbing her hands together nervously. But she didn't stand up right away. She stared ahead, feeling the need to gather a little more strength.

The view before her wasn't the Rockies—only hills New York State *called* mountains—but it was still a feast for the eyes... and a balm for the soul. From this porch she had often prayed for Toots, whose soul needed healing right now. And for her birth mother, too, whom she still hoped to find. Both miracles seemed impossible now, though Millie had lived long enough to wonder if "Surprise" might be God's middle name.

"Okay, I'm ready," she said, standing and stretching her back. "The hospital hasn't called yet, so she's still hanging on. But they warned me last night that it won't be long."

"I'm ready too." Frank replied, standing up.

In the car, Millie checked her purse. Pocket New Testament? Got it. Lotion for her mother's hands? Check. Before Frank pulled onto the road, they passed their little building with the scalloped roof and hand-painted sign: "The Shepherd's Chalet Gift Store."

"You remembered to write '*Temporarily Closed*' on the sign, right?" Millie asked him. "'*For family emergency?*'"

He nodded, trying not to show the worry on his face. Closing the store on a fall weekend would hit hard, especially since it was their only income. Pamela, basically the manager by now, was down with the flu and couldn't help.

During the twenty-minute drive to the hospital, Millie reminisced. Finding their property in the Finger Lakes—a region of farms, wineries, and "mountains" divided by long, skinny lakes—

still felt like a miracle. It was just four miles from the house Toots and Jerry had bought, which turned out to a blessing. Toots had grown weaker with age, even a bit docile, making holidays and frequent weekend dinners together possible. Even Jerry had softened, enjoying being called Dad and Grandpa now.

Yes, things had been good the last several years. In fact, it seemed like only yesterday that Toots was hobbling around her double-wide trailer, fussing with pots of geraniums and baby-talking her spoiled and consequently obese Pekingese dog.

Sure, she'd been forgetting things—harmless things at first—like how she'd recite the same poem every time you saw her. It was usually the one that began: *"I think that I shall never see a poem as lovely as a tree."*

But soon, more important things slipped away, like whether she'd taken her medicine or when she last ate.

Eventually, Alzheimer's took not only the Kilmer poem from her memory, but Millie, too.

"I'll get your door," Frank said, pulling into the hospital lot. He always opened her door anyway, but in his nervousness might've felt the need to mention it. Millie had been unusually quiet on the ride.

In the lobby, Millie turned to Frank. "Wait here. I want to talk to her alone."

Frank didn't argue. His wife had that look on her face, one he knew all too well. She wasn't giving up. She would try to get through to her mother one last time.

"I'll be praying for you," he said, sitting down in a nearby chair.

The hospice unit was a solemn place, where even the softest of steps in the hall seemed loud and the watercolor prints on the walls looked cheap and melancholy. Death wasn't in Millie's comfort zone, and like many, she hated hospitals. But today she was going to take it all in. The faint elevator music coming from the ceiling speakers. The beeping machines. The stoic nurses carrying clip-boards. *Her mother.*

"Hi, Mom," Millie whispered, pushing back a curtain. Toots lay facing the door with a row of cards and flowers behind her on the windowsill. Many of the blooms were wilted from the air vent blowing on them. Millie stepped closer and sat on the edge of the bed.

"It's me, your daughter. Can you hear me?"

No response. Toots's eyes remained closed, her seventy-seven years of proud facial history drained of all spunk and vigor. She looked so pale. So cold.

Millie gently touched her hand. "I brought your favorite lotion, the rose-scented one."

Still no response. Millie removed the bottle from her purse, squeezed out some lotion, and massaged it into Toots's hand, then up her limp, sagging arm.

Toots opened her eyes.

"Hi, Mom, it's me, Millie. Can you hear me?" she asked again.

Toots stared back vacantly. Millie took a deep breath.

"Mom, I have something to share with you. I've tried a few times before to talk to you about this, but it's important I try one last time. I've known the truth about my birth for a long time. I've known about Jeanette Coyer, and—"

She paused, unsure whether the name would spark anything. It didn't. Only her eyes blinked.

"And I also know you raised me as best as you knew how. I want to say *thank you* for that. I was often a terrible brat to you, and I'm sorry. Thank you for loving me. Thank you for doing so much to raise me as your own daughter."

Toots stirred, her face showing a flicker of discomfort.

"It's okay, Mom I'm not angry at you for not telling me. I know you were scared—scared of being rejected, scared of what revealing the truth might mean. But you don't have to be afraid. I love you. I really do."

Millie's eyes filled. She could hardly believe it. She wasn't just saying these things. *She meant them.*

Enveloping Toots's hand in hers, Millie leaned closer and softly sang the familiar hymn:

> *Amazing Grace, how sweet the sound,*
> *That saved a wretch like me.*
> *I once was lost, but now I'm found,*
> *Was blind but now I see.*
> *'Twas grace that taught my heart to fear,*
> *And grace my fears relieved.*
> *How precious did that grace appear,*
> *The hour I first believed.*

Between the stanzas, Millie noticed it: *Toots was singing.* Not audibly, but her lips were clearly mouthing the words. And the whole time, her grip on Millie's hand had tightened.

What it all meant, especially given her condition, could be debated. Millie, however, wanted to believe Toots was comprehending God's love. She wanted to believe that she was asking for God's "amazing grace" to save her and relieve her of all her fears.

A couple of weeks later, Millie shared this story at her mother's burial with some family and friends.

"I have hope," she told them. "I have hope that I'll see my mother again someday."

# CHAPTER 30

# *End of the World*

A couple of years after Toots's death, Frank, Millie, and Pamela were driving home from a Bible study they attended regularly at someone's home. Even though it was an hour each way, the drive passed quickly. There was always something to talk about.

The motley crew they met with—usually between eight and twelve people—was disorganized and sometimes off the rails entirely. It made for high-spirited, interesting evenings. Millie especially appreciated that her voice mattered. Anything could be asked, anything could be challenged, and it was all encouraged. That kind of freedom was rare; in fact, it was a gift she'd travel even farther for.

The June night was humid and sticky, with a light drizzle. The smell of frogs and earthworms on the misty asphalt drifted up into the car's cracked-open windows.

As usual, Millie felt the need to "help" Frank drive.

"Slow down! You're running over them!"

"I can't save them all. There are too many."

"You have to try. Especially the big ones. Oh, right there! Be careful!"

Millie pointed at a large hopping frog in the high beams—but Frank wasn't sure which one to swerve around. They all looked the same to him.

Pamela leaned over the back seat to assess the "frog land-mine." Her mom's love of critters could be dangerous—like the time she had pulled over on a three-lane highway to rescue a snapping turtle. Pamela and Frankie were sitting helpless in the back seat, watching as their mother dodged speeding cars and tractor-trailers to stop the traffic.

It was a terrifying sight they'd never forget.

Thankfully, this wasn't that. The frogs were numerous, but it was late and the road was quiet.

"So, what were we talking about?" Pamela asked, sitting back. She thought it best to distract her parents from the frogs. Her dad, patient as he was, sometimes lost it when being told how to drive.

Frank picked up on her intent. "The last days, right?"

"Right. Do you think Kathy was right—that the end of the world is soon?"

"I like what Karen said," he replied, swerving slightly to avoid a frog that was so large, he almost wanted to stop and bag it. He used to eat frog legs as a kid. "She said the end of the world comes for every person when they die. It's a perspective I hadn't thought of."

"Yes, but didn't Jesus talk about another time too—an event everyone would witness at once? He gave signs to look for. Like love growing cold, pride, a focus on pleasure—"

"Deceptive teachings," Millie jumped in. Not even a plague of frogs could distract her from a lively discussion. "I can't believe how people fall for them sink, line, and hooker!"

It came out of the blue, like a sizzling meteorite hitting the ground. Pamela erupted into laughter. "Oh, Mom! That was your best one yet!"

She rummaged in her purse for a pen. She'd been collecting her mother's funny sayings for years and didn't want to forget this one.*

Millie giggled uncontrollably, and even Frank—whose laughter was drier and more reserved—chuckled so long he had to wipe away tears.

"The homework looks hard this week," Pamela said once they calmed down. She was studying some notes under a book light. "I knew when it was Harry's turn to do the questions, they'd be tough."

"Yes, but," Frank said, "I don't do windows. And I *don't* do homework."

Pamela rolled her eyes. She knew that most mornings her dad was up before anyone else, sitting at the kitchen table with his Bible and a cup of Postum—or "fake coffee" as his family called it—doing his best with the questions. He didn't always fill in all the blanks, nor did he have as many grand theological insights as others. But Frank *was* sincere in his faith, and steadfast with his daily quiet time with God.

A black-and-white English Springer Spaniel who had been sleeping in the back seat sat up and stretched. Then she looked out the window and began to whine.

Peekaboo, or "Peeka," as she was called for short, was practically a person. Bible studies weren't her thing, of course, so she either stayed outside in a shady spot or waited in the car listening to music on a battery-operated radio. In the winter, Pamela dressed her in a snowsuit to keep her warm until the meeting ended.

Millie glanced back. "Isn't it amazing how Peeka knows we're almost home?"

Frank turned into their long, winding driveway and drove slowly to their cabin at the back of the property. Gravel crunched

---

* For the full list of Millie's sayings, see the website link at the end of the book.

under the tires as they passed their sleepy little store, its lawn decorations casting eerie shadows in the mist.

The store hadn't been doing well lately. *Was it something they were doing wrong? Or was it the rise of dollar stores everywhere?* While they couldn't agree on the reason, they were thankful they still had a few local customers with "green pockets," as Millie called them, who dug deep and kept them afloat.

They passed Dolly, the old mare, standing in the moonlight with her rear leg bent in her usual sleeping pose. A car was parked by the garage.

"Frankie's here for the weekend," Millie said, spotting it.

Frank pulled up beside it.

"Tomorrow we're going to work on his brakes," he said. "Once he gets up, of course."

Before bed, Millie reminded Frank about the special order he needed to finish: a life-size wooden cutout of a German Shepherd. She needed to hand-paint it to match the customer's photo.

Frank assured her it was on his list and gave her a kiss goodnight. Tomorrow would be a full day, but not stressful. Frank liked being his own boss. He liked doing different things every day.

The next morning came too soon.

"Sorry, I didn't mean to wake you," Frank whispered as Millie's eyes blinked open. "I'm just going for a walk."

Faint rays of early dawn filtered through the curtains. Frank grabbed his Roy Rogers baseball cap and walking stick from the closet.

"I'll take Peeka," he added, slipping out the door.

Millie grunted and rolled over in bed. Thankfully, Pamela was opening the store. As for Frank, he always rose with the birds. It wasn't unusual for him to be out before anyone else, walking in the woods behind the house. The trail was steep but short enough to manage. At the top he had cleared a "thinking spot" for himself, complete with a campfire ring, benches, and space for a tent.

When the digital clock read ten, Millie was still in her pajamas and puttering in the kitchen. Post-Bible-study mornings were always slow for her. She was on her second cup of coffee when the intercom crackled with static. It was Pamela. They used the two-ways as a quick way to talk between the store and the house.

"Yoo-hoo, anyone there?"

In the background, the faint sound of Appalachian music was heard.

*Good girl,* Millie thought. *She's finally putting music on first thing. Very important for ambience.*

"I'm here. What's up?"

"Is Dad there?"

"No. I thought he was helping you open the store. He went for a walk earlier, but..."

Millie's voice trailed off. She hadn't seen Frank or Peeka since getting up, and Frankie was still in his room. A sudden wave of dread tightened in her chest. Frank's mug wasn't in the sink.

*It was still hanging on the cup hook.*

"Close the store, Pam. Right now. Something's wrong."

An awakened Frankie was the first into action. He threw on his clothes, jumped on the ATV, and tore up the steep trail behind the house. Minutes later, Millie and Pamela were huffing up the path on foot, calling out.

From the top came a voice—Frankie's. "Get help! Get help!"

Pamela turned and sprinted back down the trail to call 911 from the house. While she waited there for help, Millie kept climbing the trail, her heart pounding.

*Oh God, oh God. This can't be happening.*

When she crested the hill, she saw them: Frank was lying face-up on the ground, motionless. And Frankie was giving him CPR.

In moments like this—when sudden tragedy occurs—some people say time slows down. It didn't for Millie. Time blurred, like choppy snippets from a VHS tape on fast-forward.

Clinging to Frank's body. *He's so still.* Calling his name again and again. *He's so silent.* And nearby, her son—*God bless her son* —doing all he could to save his dad, even though it had been too late by the time anyone got there.

What did crawl, however, was the next day, and the day after that. Her husband had a fatal heart attack? At the age of fifty-two? Every waking moment was numbed with disbelief. Frank was her best friend. They had weathered thirty years of storms together. Challenges with Toots. The emotional hunt for her birth mother. Chronic depression and anger. Her radical transformation in Christ, followed by another rollercoaster of walking *that* out.

Anyone else might have jumped ship. But Frank—this quiet Polish boy from Pennsylvania—was a rock. He kept loving her through everything. In fact, Millie would spend her days of grief insisting that *nobody* loved her with God's love except for Frank.

A bit pedestaled, perhaps, which might explain why she battled with such crushing guilt. Every night, she beat herself up. Every morning, she woke up bruised. All she could think about was how she'd failed to give back to Frank the love that *he* needed.

One late July night after the memorial service, it hit her especially hard. She was alone in bed. A full moon poured through the window, lighting up a stack of *Roy Rogers Show* VHS tapes in the corner—a collection Frank planned to watch when he "retired" someday. The sight of them triggered another wave of grief.

*I worked him too hard! I didn't encourage him to rest. I was too insensitive, too selfish!*

To stifle her sobs, she pressed a pillow to her face so tightly that she almost didn't want to lift it to breathe.

Then came the voice.

*"Do you want him back?"*

It filled the room, quiet but unmistakable. Millie knew who it was. The pillow slipped off the bed. She tried to speak, but the voice continued:

*"Frank is with me, Millie. He's being loved perfectly by me right now. No one on earth could love Frank like me. I am love. And Frank is fully enjoying that love."*

"Oh..." Millie exhaled, releasing weeks of pent-up pain. Relief flooded her body. Frank was with God. And God was love. She didn't need to carry the weight of guilt anymore!

It was a sacred moment, one that called for a response. Millie softly began to sing another favorite song:

*You are my hiding place,*
*Whenever I am afraid, I will trust in You.*
*Let the weak say, 'I am strong, in the strength of the Lord.'*
*I will trust in You.*

From that night on, her grief was lighter. She could accept that Frank was enjoying a place incomprehensibly better than where she was. It didn't mean the sadness was over... there would be plenty of tear-soaked pillows and lonesome days to come. But she could go on. She could trust that God was good, merciful, and not detached from her pain.

Most importantly, she could trust that God is *love*.

# CHAPTER 31

# The Hunt Resumes

"How do you spell 'like'?" Millie called out, loud enough for someone to hear. Nobody answered.

She'd been told she did this a lot: calling into an empty room as if people were waiting in the shadows to answer her beck and call. She usually believed there was... at least when it came to spell checks.

The little cuckoo clock on the wall chimed eight times. She tried again, louder this time.

"*Hello?* How do you spell 'like'?"

"L-I-K-E!" a grumpy voice yelled from down the hall.

Pamela, thirty-six and living with Millie, hated raising her voice... especially before coffee. And *especially* to spell such a ridiculously simple word.

"Thanks," Millie said. "That's what I had. It just looked funny."

She resumed slowly poking the keyboard, using one finger. Then she looked up to read what she had so far.

"*Hello, my name is Millie. I would like to share with you my story.*"

It was 2004, eight years after Frank had passed away and the first year when more homes had computers than blenders. Millie still lived in Bristol—the dream property now turning into a nightmare. Weeds and vines were overtaking the sheds. Leaks dripped from mysterious places. Every day, it seemed, something was breaking or falling apart, prodding her to consider moving. It was just that making big changes without Frank was hard. They used to do all their adventures together.

*Someday,* she told herself, *it will be the right time to sell.*

But not every change had waited for Millie. One day Pamela announced she didn't want to manage the gift shop anymore. So, Millie shut it down. Not that it was hard... after Frank passed away it seemed everybody passed by the shop anyway. Frankie had also gotten married, and both he and Pamela had started their own businesses.

Then another change came... sitting on her desk in the form of a plastic box with a screen, a keyboard, and a clicky thing called a "mouse." Without hesitation, this Christmas gift from her kids awakened a desire she thought she had buried.

*She was going to use it to find her birth mother.*

Millie stretched her achy back. Learning new technology for her was intimidating. It took her weeks just to get brave enough to turn it on. But now, to her amazement, she was typing and saving things! Well, typing everything in an "email" format, Pamela had said. Either way, her goal was clear: gather all the information she knew about her birth and Jeanette Coyer into one letter, and then—somehow—launch it into "hyperspace" for others to find.

A few more minutes passed. The only sounds in the house were clicking of keys and Punky, their sassy Maine Coon cat, chattering at birds through the sliding glass doors.

When the clock struck nine, Millie had completed a full paragraph. Then something happened.

"Oh no! Where'd my icon go?!"

Punky jumped and bolted from the room.

"Help me, Pam! Hurry! The computer broke!"

Pamela emerged from her bedroom, cranky and groggy, pulling on a bathrobe. "Seriously, Mom? I was up until three in the morning adding new products to the website and—"

"I don't care," Millie interrupted. "This is an emergency!

"What now?"

"Everything I typed is gone. I think the computer broke!"

"It didn't break. Let me sit down. And stop clicking that—it's not a hyperlink."

"What's a hyperlink?"

"Ugh, I've told you a hundred times," Pamela groaned, running a hand through her tangled hair. "It's like a door, to pages on the inter—oh, never mind. Just move."

"Fine. But maybe if you were nicer, I'd remember more of what you say."

Pamela sighed. By now, she knew patience was *not* one of her virtues.

"You just minimized your email," Pamela said, restoring the window from where it was hiding. "And your mouse batteries are low, too. See the blinking light? Your cursor will act weird when that happens."

*Minimized... cursor... hyperlink...* Millie felt like her brain was overheating.

*Why does everything have to be so darn complicated?*

SOME TIME LATER, Pamela apologized to her mother as they sat on the front porch... not just for that one incident, but for all the times she'd been impatient. There was no reason for it; her mother *had* been trying. In fact, Millie was now dabbling in discussion boards—impressive considering their complexity— and using them for ancestry research.

Frankie was on the porch too, with his wife Tammy nestled close beside him on the bench swing. They were all watching the sky put on a silent but intimidating show of heat lightning across the horizon.

"Any leads yet, Mom?" Frankie asked. "In the search for your mom?"

Millie, sitting on the second porch swing, opened her mouth to respond.

"Ooh, did you see that one?" Pamela cut in, pointing toward a lightning strike over Bristol Ski Mountain. She was sitting on the top porch step while tossing a tennis ball to Peeka.

Frustrated with her weak throw, Pamela stood up, grabbed a large wooden slingshot from a nearby hook, and launched the ball far into the field ahead. Peekaboo, driven by strong Springer instincts, dove into the spot where she thought the ball-shaped "bird" had landed. Then she bounded up and down like a deer in the tall grasses trying to find it.

"Over there, Peeka!" Millie shouted, pointing. "No, the other way!"

Peeka poked her panting head out from the edge of the field, spotted Millie's hand gesture, and bounded back in. The tall grass reminded Millie of Dolly who had to be given to a new owner. It was hard, but Millie hadn't ridden her much since Frank died, and the upkeep had become too much to handle.

"No, nothing yet," she finally answered Frankie. "But I told a friend about it. She's a whiz at genealogies and said she'd investigate. Oh! Did I tell you guys I'm talking to someone online who might be related to your dad?"

She then went on about a mysterious "skeleton in the closet" story in the Spock lineage... something about a woman, a priest, and a baby.

"Well, don't give up," Frankie said, steering things back. "The internet keeps growing. And Google just passed Yahoo in popularity. Try that."

A long silence followed. The summer green of the mountain was muted, blanketed in a strange, grayish hue. Aside from the flickers of lightning and Peeka rustling through the field, the only movement came from the silvery aspen leaves shimmering in an imperceptible breeze.

Millie felt a tinge of sentimentality. She wished Frank was on the porch with them watching the storm roll in.

"It was an afternoon like this when we buried Frank," she said, breaking the quiet. "Remember? It started off still and heavy, then by the time we got to the cemetery, it rained so hard that nobody under the tent could hear each other."

"How old were you?" Tammy asked softly. She was a gregarious, pretty girl who loved all things beautiful and positive, but she too seemed subdued.

"Forty-nine."

Tammy rested her blonde hair on Frankie's shoulder, sighing. "That's way too young to lose a husband."

Frankie pecked her on the forehead.

Millie smiled at the lovebirds, grateful for the gift of forgiveness. It was still painful to remember how, when they were dating, she and Pamela had caused them pain. If only she could always remember that kindness and mercy are the true forces of love—not fear, judgment, or control. Forgetting this can lead people to misinterpret the Bible and use it in ways it was never meant to be. When she and Pamela finally realized they were in error, their apologies came swiftly and tearfully. In time, reconciliation followed... proving that the bond of family is strong.

Her only wish now was for them to have children. At this point, though, they said they weren't planning to.

"Hey Mom," Pamela said, hanging the slingshot back on its hook. "I don't know if I ever told you this. But shortly after Dad died, I was in the basement when I heard you singing upstairs. I crept up the steps and peeked through a crack in the door. You were on your knees washing the floor and crying—tears streaming down your face—but you kept singing. I don't remember the song, exactly; some little praise tune. But I'll never forget how you carried both pain and faith at the same time. It inspired me."

Millie gave a modest smile and stood. Then she slid open the screen door. She loved watching storms, but this one was taking its sweet time. And she loved feeding people even more.

"Hungry, anyone? I made enough goulash to feed an army."

Frankie and Tammy whispered to each other, then stood. "Okay, Mom, but we'll have to eat and run. We've still got orders to fill tonight."

A pile of dirty bowls later, the storm seemed to have fizzled out. Frankie and Tammy said their goodbyes, and Pamela retreated to her office. Millie settled back into her chair but kept an eye on the strange-colored sky and the open screen door, which rattled with the occasional gust.

"Something's coming," she said, again to no one visible. "It's weird out there!"

If Millie's weather prediction was right, it would be pouring soon and she'd have to rush to slide a bucket under the newest leak from the skylight.

What she couldn't have predicted, however, was what would come with the rain.

*God wasn't finished with his surprises.*

# CHAPTER 32

# Surprised by God

E ver since coupons became a thing, Millie had been a clipper. Every Sunday evening, like any proper "coupon queen," she could be found enthroned in her recliner with scissors in one hand and newspaper inserts in the other. She couldn't bear the thought of buying even a gumball without a coupon. It was all part of a game she loved—whether at yard sales, restaurants, or anywhere else. Getting a good deal was in her blood.

That evening when the long-awaited rain finally came, it was clipping time. Coupons covered Millie's armrests, lap, and the coffee table. *America's Funniest Home Videos* played in the background when suddenly a wind gust blew through the screen door.

"No! No, no!" Millie cried, scrambling to save the scattering piles. "Pam, did you shut the windows like I asked? It's raining!"

She jumped up to shut the door, sending even more coupons flying. Just then the phone rang. She grabbed the handset and fumbled with the buttons.

"How do you answer this stupid—oh, hello?"

"Hi Millie, it's Anne, Anne VanPatten. Um, did I catch you at a bad time?"

"Oh, hi Anne. No, it's fine. I just can't get used to these new phones, you know. I miss my corded one."

"Gotcha," Anne said. "Well... you might want to sit down. I finally have some news about your birth mother."

Millie's heart skipped a beat. Anne was a new friend she and Pamela had met at a house church conference—a spunky woman with a nose for a good story. She also had skills. As soon as she had caught wind of the "Millie mystery," she went straight to work.

"Hold on," Millie said, grabbing the remote to turn off the TV. She could tell this was big. *"Pam, come here!* I'm putting this on speakerphone, Anne. I want Pam to hear this too."

Pamela came over and helped her mom find the speaker button. Anne continued.

"Okay, keep in mind I still have more digging to do, but I found information on Jeanette Coyer. The spelling is different from what you were told, Millie, and her birth year was off, too. But she was living in Rochester the year you were born, and for other reasons I'm certain it's her. But—"

"But?" Millie leaned forward.

Anne sighed. "I'm terribly sorry, Millie. She passed away nine months ago in Florida. She was seventy-seven... the same age Mildred was when she died."

Millie's shoulders slumped. She had always known this was a possibility—*but just nine months ago?* She tried to remember what she'd been doing then. Something important? Why hadn't she searched harder? Found Anne sooner?

Anne continued. "There's more. Jeanette had a sister who's still alive—and believe it or not she lives in Rochester. I have her phone number if you want it."

Millie gestured for Pamela to write the number down. After the call, she took the scrap of paper and began dialing.

"I'd better do this now," she said, taking a deep breath, "before I chicken out."

A woman answered.

"Hi, is this Rosemary?" Millie asked, her voice cracking. "My name is Millie. You don't know me but... did you had a sister named Jeanette Coyer?"

Pamela sat nearby, listening quietly. The call was no longer on speaker, so she could only hear her mother's side.

"So, you're not sure if she had a baby in 1947?" Millie said, frowning. "Uh-huh... yes, I understand."

Then, suddenly, a memory surfaced. "Wait. By chance, did Jeanette have bowed legs? She did? Oh, yes, that's *definitely* a good sign!"

There was a pause. Millie listened, then her expression turned to shock. "What? Really? Oh my goodness. Would you know how to contact any of them?"

Names and numbers were exchanged—with Pamela scribbling notes. Millie made plans to visit Rosemary in a few days and hung up the phone, her face glowing as if she'd just won the Mega Millions.

"You're not going to believe this, Pam," she gasped, clutching her head. "I have a family as big as Texas!"

The rest of the evening unfolded like Christmas morning. Millie called the first number on her list—a woman named Candace in central Florida. Midway through the opening sentence, Candace interrupted her.

"Hold on. I want the others to hear this!"

Voices erupted in the background. Then a woman screeched over the line, "Oh my God, Millie? Is that really you? I can't believe it—after all these years!"

Incidentally, four of Millie's siblings—two sisters and two brothers—were in the house at that moment. But there was more.

Jeanette went on to have *nine* more children after Millie, some of whom knew about her and had been trying to find her!

After making plans for a family reunion by the end of the month, Millie hung up the phone. She was so worked up that she spent the rest of the evening pacing the house and chattering nonstop. Her heart ached for the mother she'd never known, but it also swelled with a joy she never expected.

She had a family!

A *really big* family!

# CHAPTER 33

## A Horde of Hugs

"Ouch!" Millie winced. "Didn't you see the pothole?"

"I'm trying," Pamela said, adjusting the Garmin on the dash. The device was an unexpected perk in their rental car, but she wasn't used to it yet.

"So, we're looking for a farm stand at the corner of County Road 5 and... what was it again? Green Holler Road? I wish this thing talked. I heard some GPS's do that now."

"Yes, Green Holler," Millie said, checking a piece of paper in her hand. "Glenn said it would be easier to find Candace's place if we followed him. Oh, wait! Is that him?"

She pointed to a corner lot with a rundown shack and a faded "Boiled Peanuts" sign with several missing letters. Next to the sign, a man lounged on a motorcycle.

"That must be him," Millie said. "Ooh, look at that panhandle mustache! He's just like I imagined him!"

"Panhandle?" Pamela repeated, looking confused. She eased the car onto the cracked asphalt lot, parking next to the motorcycle.

Millie fumbled for the door handle, breathless. Meanwhile, the man approached the car. He wore tattered jeans, a sleeve-less T-shirt, and sported both a long mustache and a gray ponytail.

"Hiya, Sis!" he said as Millie stepped out. Then he pulled her into a bear hug with his muscular, tattooed arms.

She squealed. "Oh, it's wonderful to finally meet you, brother Glenn! I just can't believe it!"

*I just can't believe it.* Millie had said this phrase a hundred times since finding her family. She had said it when meeting her new aunt Rosemary and cousin Johnny in Rochester for the first time. She had said it while planning to attend her first Coyer reunion in Florida. And she would say it again today, a dozen more times.

"Ready?" Glenn asked, swinging his leg over the seat and kicking back the stand. "The chain gang is waiting."

With Glenn leading the way, they began their slow trek to Candace's house. The loose, sandy road was lined with saw palmettos and cacti as abundant as grass up north. Some houses looked barely habitable, and a couple of times Pamela had to swerve around chickens in the road.

Millie was captivated by the sight of a lemon tree in someone's yard, its branches heavy with ripe fruit.

"People are so lucky to have lemon trees here," she said with a sigh. "I wish they grew up north."

Pamela glanced over.

"When life gives you lemons..." she prompted.

"...keep them," Millie grinned. "Because they're *free lemons!*"

This was a line from a fridge magnet her kids gave her as a joke. Everyone knew Millie loved lemons, and she wasn't shy about asking for extra slices—sometimes even a whole cup of them—for her water at restaurants.

They finally arrived at Candace's home, a newer double-wide trailer nestled among ferns and the shade of towering "Live Oaks," as they were strangely called. As Glenn's motorcycle rumbled to a stop, the gate swung open and a crowd of people surrounded the car before Millie could open her door.

A woman with pensive blue eyes was the first to embrace her.

"I'm your sister, Penny," she said kindly into Millie's ear.

Three men followed behind her, holding beers and grinning widely. They introduced themselves as Ralph, Mickey, and Greg—the youngest who was just a few years older than Pamela.

Another woman took Millie's arm and rubbed it affectionately. It was Beverly.

"Oh, look at her arms!" she exclaimed. "And her hands too! They're just like Mom's!"

"You definitely look like Mom," Candace said when it was her turn for a hug.

Millie was struck by how much she resembled this sister—the second oldest. In fact, she saw bits of herself in all of them. It just hadn't occurred to her how she might, as the firstborn, bear an especially strong resemblance of Jeanette in their eyes.

As she and Pamela followed everyone into the yard, Millie murmured a silent prayer.

*May I be a comfort to them, Lord. May each of these precious people come to know you and your love more closely!*

"You women can cackle in the henhouse. We roosters will tend the grills," Mickey teased, cracking open a beer. Peeking from a baby sling on his chest was a trembling chihuahua.

Mickey was clearly the family jester... and smitten with his dog.

The women went inside to chat in the bug-free, air-conditioned living room. In the kitchen nearby, casserole dishes and cold salads lined the counters. Soon, Ralph brought in trays of grilled chicken and sausages.

Millie carried a plate of food back to her chair but only picked at it. She was too full of questions and curiosity.

One of the first things she learned was that her mother had ten children by a few different fathers. Unfortunately, no one knew who Millie's father was, and—for specific reasons—they were certain he wasn't one of theirs.

"But even though we don't all share the same father," Candace said, tightening her embrace around a squirming granddaughter, "we're a pretty tight-knit family. Mom always wanted that."

"Yes," Beverly added, sitting next to Millie. She leaned over and placed a hand on Millie's arm. "Mom wasn't one to give up on any of her kids. We know she wanted you."

Millie's breath caught. She long believed that... but hearing it from someone who knew Jeanette was a gift.

"Bev is right," Candace said, letting her granddaughter go play. "Every January around your birthday, Mom would drink too much and cry, mumbling your name. That's how we first learned of you. When we got older and a couple of us asked her about it, she explained that you were her first baby."

Millie swallowed hard, fighting back tears. "That's so sad. Did she say what happened between her and the woman who raised me? Her name was Mildred, by the way. She named me after herself. Jeanette lived with her for almost a year after I was born."

Beverly answered. "Unfortunately, not much. I tried to encourage mom to open up... thought it would help. I even suggested writing to *Unsolved Mysteries* for her, hoping they might find you. But she'd change the subject and retreat into her secret. It was like she was afraid of something."

Millie sighed, placing her glass on a nearby end table. The thought of what Jeanette must have gone through was heartbreaking. Penny walked over and filled her glass with more sweet tea.

"Other than that," Candace said, "I don't think we know much more than you do, Millie. Although Mom once said something that gave us the impression you were 'taken' from her—but that's about it."

Millie took this as her cue. She reached into her purse and pulled out copies of the magazine article that Aunt Ethel had first shown her. Her friend Anne had found it on microfiche at the Rochester Public Library. As her siblings skimmed the copies she passed around, Millie tried to summarize.

"Basically, someone—I don't know who—claimed theft happened when I was taken from Jeanette and given to Mildred. They wrote a letter to the magazine editor, hoping it would help. But I fell through the cracks somehow. Plus, Mildred wanted everyone to believe she gave birth to me, even managing an illegal birth certificate. I suspected things while never having the whole truth."

Penny, seated across from Millie, read her copy with wide eyes. The room was silent except for the rattle of a small window air conditioner.

"Wow," she finally said, lowering the paper. "Mysteries aside, we're so glad you found us!"

Millie looked around at all the warm, welcoming faces—people who had no hesitation to receive her as family (including a couple other siblings she had not met yet). But in their kind eyes she also saw hints of pain, as if they had their own share of hardships.

What untold stories did *they* have? Had Millie's upbringing as an only child been more difficult than theirs? She'd grown up lonely, but did any of these nine siblings ever feel lost among so many?

It was a strange thought... one that filled Millie with compassion.

*Should I tell them now?* she wondered. She only paused for a moment. *How could I keep the most important part of my story to myself?*

When the moment felt right, she took a deep breath and began.

"Mildred couldn't bear children," she said. "She was also turned down for adopting. So, I grew up an only child, alone in my room a lot. Back then, I would've given my eye candy to have a family like this!"

"Eye candy?" Glenn said, sauntering in. He puffed his chest. "You talkin' about me?"

Millie laughed. "Sure am—about all of us! We're all precious to God. But until my late twenties, I didn't believe that for myself. I let shame and anger rule my life, even though I had a loving husband and two beautiful children."

She glanced at Pamela, who offered a small smile.

"But one day Jesus Christ changed me," Millie continued, her face lighting up. She always sparkled when she shared this part of her story. "I was all alone, with no one around to pray for me or say any rites. I just cried out to God to make himself real to me in whatever way I needed. And he did! All the 'yuck' was washed out of me, from the top of my head to the tips of my toes!"

Millie lifted her foot, clad in a pink sock and white slipper. The room rippled with gentle laughter. She tucked it back under her chair.

"It's like the hymn, you know, Amazing Grace? 'I was blind but now I see. I was lost but now I'm found.'"

A few of the siblings nodded and smiled. Millie's heart lifted. Had God made himself real to some of them, too?

It was an encouraging thought—beyond knowing who their mother was—to also know they were children of the same heavenly Father.

# CHAPTER 34

## Golden Years

With her back hunched, Millie walked along the edge of her house sprinkling something on the ground. It wasn't her home in Bristol—the one with the gift shop and acres of land. She had finally accepted it was time to let go of that property, along with the mountain where Frank had passed.

Her new home required less maintenance and was conveniently located in town. It was also overrun with stray cats.

Pamela pulled into the driveway and stepped out of her pickup truck. As she came up the path, she weaved around a trail of paper plates licked clean by the cats.

"What are you doing?" she asked.

"Sprinkling popcorn crumbs," Millie said.

"Why are you doing that?"

"To feed the mice."

Pamela blinked. "Are you serious? Don't you know that will draw rats?"

Millie shrugged. "Whatever. Then I'm feeding the 'possums instead!"

Pamela chuckled as she passed her mother.

"Where are you going?" Millie asked. "I'm ready to go. We have a long drive to Rochester."

"I need to use your bathroom first, and we've got time. We don't have to pick up that dresser until two and it's only a thirty-minute drive."

Millie gathered the plates and followed her, waiting in the kitchen. She lingered by the fridge to straighten a photo of Max and Spencer—her beloved grandsons—held up by a ladybug magnet.

*Are they really ten and eight already?* she thought to herself. It seemed like only yesterday that Frankie and Tammy had made the joyful announcement that they were starting a family after all.

Her gaze drifted to a another photo of her siblings with her in the center grinning from ear to ear. In the decade since their first reunion, Millie had stayed close to all of them, even making a solo trip to Florida to spend time with them. Her brother Glenn had visited her in New York a few times, too, and they were always amazed by how naturally they felt connected... like they had never spent their childhoods apart.

She turned toward the breakfast nook and smiled. In the center of the table sat a bouquet of hand-picked wildflowers from yet another unexpected blessing in her life... a fiancé!

"Imagine that", she whispered, sliding the vase toward her. "I'm almost seventy and getting married!"

She gently removed the wilted stems, leaving only the freshest.

"Are those from Bill?" Pamela asked, rounding the corner. "They're pretty."

Millie grabbed her purse and slung it over her shoulder, still holding the faded flowers.

"Uh-huh," she answered curtly. "Come on. Let's hit the road."

Before getting into the truck, she dropped the wilted blooms along the driveway and brushed some soil over them with the toe of her shoe. She thought of her mother, Jeanette, who she'd been told used to do the same thing—never discarding cut flowers in the trash, but instead giving them a second chance to reseed.

*Was this an inherited habit?* Millie wondered. *Despite having spent such a short time as a baby with Jeanette, could small peculiarities like that be passed down through blood and time?*

Aside from the GPS speaking directions, the ride to Rochester was quiet. Pamela had asked a question, but Millie was staring out the window lost in thought.

"Yoo-hoo," Pamela said a little louder. "Earth to Mom."

Millie turned her head.

"So, what do you think?" Pamela asked again, a twinkle in her eye. "Should we write your story someday?"

Millie returned a small smile; it wasn't the first time the idea had come up. A story like hers would make... well, a good story. Her mind was just elsewhere. They were on their way to Rochester to pick up a dresser Frankie had found on Craigslist, one that perfectly matched her bedroom set. She was going to need the extra storage space for a man's clothes... no, her *husband's* clothes!

She felt giddy at the thought.

"My story isn't over until the fat lady stops singing," she answered with a giggle—immediately realizing the spin she'd put on that saying. "I mean, seriously, Pam, who would've ever imagined I'd be getting married again?"

It was true—no one had imagined it. But in all her years as a widow, Millie had lived boldly and fully. She had poured all her energy into her grandsons and siblings. She had joined the Red Cross, traveling to weather-beaten states to provide aid. She had been active in a cat rescue organization. She had flown across the world to Ethiopia to visit a sponsored child through Compassion International. Even her hobbies were gutsy and interesting: from fossil digging to buying and selling antiques and collectibles.

At an age when most people slowed down, Millie sped up—and

all the while continuing to rescue ladybugs and care for them in a ladybug house!

Of course, there had been disappointments, too—one that was still raw. Letting go and entrusting it to God was a struggle. Even after many healings and victories, Millie still carried tender places in her heart. Trusting God, especially when it involved her children, was an almost unbearable weight for her to carry.

Millie learned in this season, however, new ways to stretch her faith. She began journaling, something she'd never felt drawn to do before, and reading the Bible with a fresh fervor, finding comfort in its timeless wisdom. She even wrote that she was starting to feel "born again, *again!*"

It was also during this time that she reconnected with Bill Rider, a respected family friend. The engagement surprised everyone—not because it was Bill (most people had always thought they'd make a great couple), but that each of them had opened their hearts to love and marriage again.

After picking up the dresser, Pamela took an alternate route back through the city.

Millie perked up at a traffic light.

"Oh, look," she said, pointing to a familiar brick building. "That's the high school I walked to every day!"

She grinned. "On the days I went, that is."

At the next light, she pointed to a McDonald's.

"Somewhere around there was an ice cream parlor. I used to go to it with Nellie and Patrick. It was next to a pet shop where I stole baby turtles."

Pamela smiled; she'd always loved that story. It was an endearing example of her mom's bold, rescuing spirit.

"Make your next left," Millie said, "On Webster Avenue. I want to drive by my old house."

Pamela turned down the street lined with small 1920s cookie-cutter houses. Many had seen better days. Some were in disrepair and a few even torn down.

"There it is!" Millie said, pointing. "The white one, on the right. Pull in the driveway."

Not wanting to alarm the homeowners, Pamela parked at the curb. Millie rolled down the window for a better look. The small house sat on a corner across from an empty dirt lot where a playground used to be—now littered with soda cans and a faded realtor's sign.

As the truck idled, Millie looked up.

"There's my bedroom window," she said softly. "I spent so much time up there."

Then her expression lifted. "But look at it now. The window, the house... it all looks so small!"

She sat quietly, reflecting. The hardships she'd endured in that house were behind her now, tucked into the pages of fading memories and healed-over wounds. After many years she had emerged, not as a woman defined by her past, but as one graced to live a full, overcoming life.

"Ready to go?" Pamela asked, putting the truck in gear.

Millie rolled up the window.

"Yes, I'm ready," she said, her voice strong and resolute.

Millie was no longer the girl in the attic.

# *Epilogue*

Millie dabbed her favorite perfume behind her ears, then onto the wrists of her well-manicured, liver-spotted hands. White Diamonds, some say, is the perfect fragrance for a woman who "embodies vintage charm and class." The description suited Millie well in this mature season of life. Graceful, poised, yet still carrying a spark of youthful fire.

She stepped back to view herself in the full-length mirror. Her formal, beige-colored dress wasn't a wedding gown, but its abundance of lace made up for it. On her head she wore a dainty headband with a spray of baby's breath flowers and her matching necklace and earrings purchased at Walmart were, as always, sparkly.

*He says I'm beautiful,* Millie said to herself, smiling. It was a wonderful feeling, especially at her age, to feel that way with a man. Not that she didn't know deep down her true worth to God.

Sometimes she even recalled the little button given to her many years ago—the one that read: "I'm OK, God doesn't make junk." Although she didn't believe it back then, the little girl inside Millie resonated with its simple truth. It came at a point in time when she needed the encouragement. Later, when she experienced the love of

Jesus in a more personal way—a love that took him to the Cross—it really drove the truth home.

Millie always knew her value after that.

Still standing in front of the mirror, she turned to the side. Then she inhaled and straightened her posture. It was obvious: she'd gotten much thinner over the last few years. She was pleased with the weight loss, especially now, but it was a little concerning. She hadn't changed her diet or activity level, and even her strength was quickly fading.

Her family and Bill were worried, but she always brushed off their concerns.

"I'm a complicated case," she told them. "Even the doctors can't agree.'

Then she'd assure them, saying, "I have it under control."

Though she didn't... not really. Every doctor visit brought new and conflicting numbers. Millie just wanted to manage things her own way without getting extreme. Spending money and time she didn't have, or popping lots of pharmaceutical pills, just wasn't her style.

*It's no time to worry,* she firmly told her reflection. *God will give me strength to face whatever comes.*

Then she turned from the mirror to wait for Bill who would be arriving any minute to pick her up.

June 8<sup>TH</sup> 2017 was a spectacular day for celebrating the union of Millie Spock and Bill Rider. It sparkled with sun, warmth, and a bright blue sky. Frankie and Tammy hosted the ceremony on their spacious back deck, overlooking a view of the Bristol Hills. It was simple, lovely, and attended by a small group of close family.

After the wedding, one of Millie's dreams came true. She and

Bill went on a Caribbean cruise for their honeymoon. They visited several islands, indulged in endless food, and enjoyed all the fun and frivolity cruises are known for.

When Pamela saw them after their return, her mother was glowing.

"I'm so happy!" Millie told her, her voice gleeful as a teenager's. Then she went on to share some things that only two close friends would talk about. It was a special moment that gave Pamela a measure of relief. Much of her mother's emotional pain in recent years had been, sadly, because of her—and this was an encouraging sign that Millie's heart was healing and that their bond remained strong.

By this time Millie and Bill had settled into their home and were adjusting nicely. They also began dreaming about the future, including finding a different house together and visiting Millie's relatives, many of whom Bill hadn't yet met.

As they dreamed, however—and even earlier on the cruise itself —Millie began to experience troubling symptoms. At first, they were mild dizzy spells which she attributed to being on a boat. Back on land she blamed a new blood pressure medication she had reluctantly agreed to take.

A few months into marriage, the symptoms worsened. Millie could no longer convince everyone her health issues were "nothing." She was finally admitted to a hospital for tests, where it was discovered she had been experiencing "mini strokes" originating in a complex part of her brain. Not only were they difficult to detect... they were even more difficult to recover from.

Given the gravity of her situation, Millie gathered her family at home after her hospital stay. Though her speech was halting, she did her best to share her final wishes, apologies, and heart-felt affirmations.

Meanwhile, Pamela moved into the house to help her and Bill, unaware of how little time remained for her mother. By month's end, even swallowing became difficult, and she was readmitted to the hospital.

It was there that the doctors made the heartbreaking announcement: Millie was terminal.

Yet from God's perspective Millie's life wasn't ending. Through every season he had either carried or guided his daughter, *and he would do so again.* Death was simply the next step—a big step—on her journey to complete freedom and belonging.

When the time came, Millie clung tightly to God's hand. To those around her she showed no fear—only a bold, peaceful resolve to go on her own terms. From her hospital bed she gestured toward the feeding tubes and clearly signaled: *"Take them out."* Then, with a steady hand she pointed upward, her face alight with the confidence of someone who knew where she was going.

For those of us on this side of eternity, we will never know what Millie saw a few days later—the moment she stepped from this world into the next.

Was it the risen Jesus standing in front of the "Old Rugged Cross," like the one she had gazed on with childlike wonder in her cousins' backyard?

Was it her mother Jeanette, or Toots, *or both*—souls quickened by mercy just as hers had been?

Or was a whole *multitude* of the redeemed—*a family beyond number*—arms wide, hearts open, welcoming her into the Father's embrace?

Whatever—or whoever it was—it brought a quick gasp of wonder to her lips.

*Millie was home.*

*"Oh God,*
*from your sacred home*
*you take care of orphans*
*and widows.*
*You find families*
*for those who are lonely*
*and protect widows.*
*You set prisoners free,*
*and let them prosper."*

*Psalm 68:5-6*
*Contemporary English Version*

~

### You Can Know

When you find yourself dancing,
when you're hearing no music,
you can know — you're bubbling with divine joy.

When you hear yourself singing,
when your heart is breaking,
you can know — you're expressing true worship.

When you feel yourself loving,
when you're being treated with spite,
you can know — you're manifesting Christ's love.

When you sense yourself resting,
when you're doing what has to be done,
you can know — you're living in God's peace.

~

A POEM MILLIE WROTE LATER IN LIFE,
FOUND SCRIBBLED ON A PIECE OF PAPER,
WITH PAMELA SPOCK

*Millie – Ethiopia 2007. With Kalem, her Sponsored child*

All royalties for **Out of the Attic** are donated to
Compassion International, a non-profit child
sponsorship and humanitarian organization.
For more information, visit:
www.PamSpock.com/Transparency-Report

For photographs, records, and other information
pertaining to Millie's life story, see:
www.PamSpock.com/Out-of-the-Attic

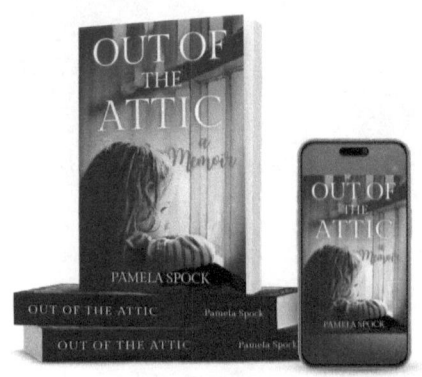

Dear Reader,
Did you enjoy Out of the Attic?
If so, would you kindly leave a review?
It would be greatly appreciated,
and also help others to find it. :-)

Blessings - Pamela

www.ingramcontent.com/pod-product-compliance
Lightning Source LLC
Chambersburg PA
CBHW030919120626
46554CB00001B/204